Easy Works for Windows™

Shelley O'Hara

Easy Works for Windows
Copyright © 1992 by Que® Corporation

All rights reserved. Printed in the United States of America. No part of this book may be used or reproduced in any form or by any means, or stored in a database or retrieval system, without prior written permission of the publisher except in the case of brief quotations embodied in critical articles and reviews. Making copies of any part of this book for any purpose other than your own personal use is a violation of United States copyright laws. For information, address Que Corporation, 11711 N. College Ave., Carmel, IN 46032.

Library of Congress Catalog No.: 92-61303

ISBN: 1-56529-063-1

This book is sold *as is*, without warranty of any kind, either express or implied, respecting the contents of this book, including but not limited to implied warranties for the book's quality, performance, merchantability, or fitness for any particular purpose. Neither Que Corporation nor its dealers or distributors shall be liable to the purchaser or any other person or entity with respect to any liability, loss, or damage caused or alleged to have been caused directly or indirectly by this book.

94 93 92   6 5 4 3 2 1

Interpretation of the printing code: the rightmost double-digit number is the year of the book's printing; the rightmost single-digit number, the number of the book's printing. For example, a printing code of 92-1 shows that the first printing of the book occurred in 1992.

Screen reproductions in this book were created using Collage Plus from Inner Media, Inc., Hollis, NH.

Publisher: Lloyd J. Short

Associate Publisher: Rick Ranucci

Project Development Manager: Thomas Bennett

Book Design: Scott Cook, Karen A. Bluestein

Production Team: Paula Carroll, Michelle Cleary, Jerry Ellis, Bob LaRoche, Dennis Sheehan, Sue VandeWalle, Johnna VanHoose, Mary Beth Wakefield, Christine Young

Credits

Production Editor
Cindy Morrow

Technical Editor
Lisa Riddle

Novice Reviewer
Stacey Beheler

Microsoft Windows is a trademark, and Microsoft Works is a registered trademark of Microsoft Corporation.

Contents at a Glance

Introduction 1

The Basics 15

Task/Review 37

Reference 221

Index 237

Contents

Introduction 1

What Is Works for Windows? 2

Why You Need This Book 8

How This Book Is Organized 8

How To Use This Book 9

How To Follow an Exercise 12

Where To Get More Help 12

The Basics 15

Understanding Your Computer System 16

Using a Mouse 18

Using Your Keyboard 19

    The Function Keys 21

    Shortcut Keys 21

    Arrow Keys 21

    Other Special Keys 23

Understanding the Tools 23

Understanding the Document Window 25

Working with Windows 28

    Closing the Window 29

    Moving and Resizing the Window 30

    Maximizing the Window 30

    Scrolling the Window 30

Selecting a Menu Command 31

Moving the Insertion Point 34

Saving and Retrieving Your Work 34

Contents

Task/Review 37

    Alphabetical Listing of Tasks 38

    Getting Started 41

        Start Works for Windows 42

        Select a tool 44

        Get help 46

        Create a new document 48

        Switch document windows 50

        Arrange document windows 52

        Close a document window 54

        Exit Works for Windows 56

    Word Processing 59

        Create a document 60

        Type text 62

        Insert text 64

        Insert a blank line 66

        Combine paragraphs 68

        Enter a page break 70

        Select text 72

        Delete text 74

        Copy text 76

        Move text 78

        Use Undo 80

        Boldface text 82

        Italicize text 84

        Underline text 86

        Change the font 88

        Change the font size 90

Contents

Center text 92

Indent text 94

Check spelling 96

Search for text 100

Replace text 102

Save a document 106

Open a document 108

Preview a document 110

Print a document 112

Spreadsheet 115

Create a spreadsheet 116

Enter text 118

Enter a number 120

Enter a date 122

Enter a formula 124

Use a function 126

Edit a cell entry 128

Erase a cell entry 130

Copy a cell entry 132

Move a cell entry 134

Select a range 136

Copy a range 138

Clear a range 140

Move a range 142

Copy a formula 144

Set column width 146

Align text 148

Format a range 150

Contents

    Make an entry bold 152

    Insert a column 154

    Delete a column 156

    Insert a row 158

    Delete a row 160

    Save a spreadsheet 162

    Open a spreadsheet 164

    Preview a spreadsheet 166

    Print a spreadsheet 168

Database 171

    Create a database 172

    Add a label 174

    Enter a field name 176

    Add a field 178

    Edit a field name 180

    Move a field 182

    Change the size of a field 184

    Delete a field 186

    Save a database 188

    Open a database 190

    Enter a record in form view 192

    Add a record in form view 194

    Display a record in form view 196

    Edit a record in form view 198

    Find a record in form view 200

    Delete a record in form view 202

    Change to list view 204

Contents

Change the field width 206

Add a record in list view 208

Edit a record in list view 210

Delete a record in list view 212

Sort records 214

Preview a database 216

Print a database 218

Reference 221

Quick Reference Guide 222

   Word Processor 222

   Spreadsheet 225

   Database 227

Keyboard Guide 230

   To open a menu 230

   To select a menu command 230

   To select a text box in a dialog box 230

   To select a check box or option button
     in a dialog box 230

   To select an item in a list box 230

   To select text 231

   To select cells in a spreadsheet 231

Glossary 231

Index 237

Introduction

What Is Works for Windows?

Why You Need This Book

How This Book Is Organized

How To Use This Book

How To Follow an Exercise

Where To Get More Help

Easy Works for Windows

Introduction

What Is Works for Windows?

Works for Windows is an integrated program that combines many tools (word processing, drawing, spreadsheet, charting, and database features) into one easy-to-use program. You can use these tools to create a variety of documents. This book covers the three main tools: the word processor, the spreadsheet, and the database.

The word processing tool enables you to create the following types of documents:

- Letters
- Memos
- Reports
- Manuscripts
- Press releases
- Legal documents
- Form letters

Open House
Sunday July 19
8505 Westfield Blvd.

Your dream house is for sale. This country-style farm house has been updated for all modern conveniences, but also retains country charm. Five huge bedrooms, including a master suite, and three full baths make this charmer ideal for any family. Sip lemonade on the wrap-around porch. Sunbathe by the outdoor swimming pool. Throw parties in the entertainment room. You won't believe all this house has to offer: three-car garage, dining room with built-in corner cabinets, country kitchen, two fireplaces.

Kimberly Moore, Listing Agent.

The spreadsheet tool enables you to create the following types of documents:

Expenses

	January	February	March	April	May
Travel	300	350	300	425	400
Advertisements	45	55	40	75	100
Flyers	50	25	25	50	75
Newsletter	75	75	75	75	75
Gifts	200	250	300	250	200
Total	$670.00	$755.00	$740.00	$875.00	$850.00

- Home budget
- Business budget
- Sales report
- Business expense report
- Financial report
- Check register

The database tool enables you to create the following types of documents:

- Inventory reports
- Invoice reports
- Personnel reports
- Client listings

Personal Financial Statement

Date	7/1/92
Assets	
Cash (checking accounts)	$2,500
Cash (savings accounts)	$5,000
Certificates of deposit	$3,000
Cash value of life insurance	$35,000
Real Estate (market value)	$135,000
Vehicles (market value)	$35,000
401Ks	$15,000
Total Assets	**$230,500**
Liabilities	
Current bills	$5,000
Mortgages	$90,000
Loans	$25,000
Taxes	$5,000
Other	$3,000
Total Liabilities	**$128,000**
Net Worth	**$102,500**

You can create these same documents manually. For instance, you can create letters, memos, and reports with a typewriter. You can create budgets and other financial documents with column-ruled paper and a calculator. You can file invoices or employee records on paper. But Works makes creating these documents easier.

	LAST NAME	FIRST NAME	DEPARTMENT	EMPLOYEE CODE
1	Cady	Barb	Marketing	D101
2	Hanley	T.L.	Sales	A104
3	Hodge	Kelly	Sales	A103
4	Marbaugh	Kathleen	Sales	A102
5	McCalley	Chris	Sales	A106
6	Paynter	Barb	Sales	A101
7	Schmutte	Steve	Marketing	D102
8	Sullivan	Kelley	Human Resources	C101
9	Wagner	Pam	Management	B101
10	Ward	Dan	Management	B102
11	Worcester	Ann	Human Resources	C102
12				
13				
14				
15				
16				
17				
18				
19				
20				
21				
22				
23				
24				
25				
26				
27				
28				
29				
30				
31				
32				
33				
34				
35				
36				
37				
38				
39				
40				
41				
42				
43				
44				
45				
46				
47				
48				
49				
50				
51				

The word processing tool lets you perform the following tasks:

Correct errors. With a typewriter, after you press a key, that letter is committed to paper. To correct a mistake, you have to use correction fluid or retype the document.

With Works, you see the text on-screen. You can easily correct any typographical errors before you print the document.

```
                        MEMO
TO:        All employees

FROM:      Stacey Ann

DATE:      7/13/92

SUBJECT:   Company picnic

The Company picnic will be held on Saturday, July 18 at Deercreek Park from 1PM to
6PM. Food, beverages, and entertainment will be provided. All you need to bring is your
family.

For directions to the park, stop by my office. See you Saturday!
```

Move around quickly. With the document on-screen, you can move from one sentence, one paragraph, or one page to another. You can quickly move from the top of the document to the bottom and vice versa.

Make editing changes. You can insert text into any location in your document. You can also quickly delete text—a character, a word, a sentence, a paragraph, or any amount of text.

Rearrange your text. When you sit down to write, you don't always write in order—from the introduction to the summary. Ideas might occur to you in a different order. As you're writing the summary, for example, you might think of an idea that belongs in the introduction. Works lets you easily move and copy text from one location in the document to another.

Restore deleted text. When you accidentally delete text that you want to keep, you don't have to retype it. Instead, you can simply restore the text.

Check spelling. Before you print, you can run a spelling check to search for misspellings. If you are a poor typist, you can leave spelling errors for Works to catch so that you can concentrate on writing instead of spelling.

Search for text. You can search your document for a particular word or phrase. For example, you can move quickly to the section of your document that discusses expenditures by searching for the word *expenditures*.

Search and replace text. You can make replacements throughout the document quickly and easily. For example, you can change all occurrences of the word *Speaker* to *Presenter* in a document.

Make formatting changes. With Works, you can easily change margins, tabs, and other formatting options. You can experiment with the settings until the document appears as you want it. Then you can print the document.

Change how text is printed. You can make text bold or italic. You can also use a different font (typeface), provided that your printer supports the use of different fonts.

Preview your document. You can preview your document to see how it will look when you print it. If you need to make changes, you can make them before you print.

The spreadsheet tool lets you perform the following tasks:

Calculate quickly and accurately. One advantage of creating your spreadsheets in Works is how easily you can write simple formulas to add, subtract, multiply, and divide. You tell Works what numbers to use, and you can depend on Works to calculate the results correctly every time.

Make changes and recalculate automatically. You can change, add, or delete data, and Works will recalculate results automatically. You do not need to erase and rewrite when you forget a crucial figure, and you don't have to manually recalculate all the amounts when you do make a change or an addition.

Rearrange data. With your spreadsheet on-screen, you can add or delete a column or row of data. You can copy and move data from one spot to another.

Repeat information. You can copy text, a value, or a formula to another place in the spreadsheet. For instance, in your monthly budget spreadsheet, you total the expenses for each month. You can write a formula that calculates January's totals, for example, and then copy this formula for February through December.

Change the format of data. You can format your results in many ways. You can tell Works to display a number with dollar signs, as a percent, or as a date. You can tell Works to align text left, right, or center.

Add enhancements. The heart of the spreadsheet tool is its number-crunching capabilities, but the results are what you use. In addition to controlling how data is displayed, you can call attention to certain results by adding shading, underlining data, and outlining data, for instance.

The database tool lets you perform the following tasks:

Change records. If a client moves or an invoice changes, you don't have to create a new form. You can easily update the existing record on-screen.

Find records quickly. Rather than sort through many paper records, you can use the database tool to pull up the record you want instantly.

Sort records. You can sort the records in the database in many different ways. For instance, you can sort a client list in ZIP code order so that mailings are easier to compile. You can sort a phone list in alphabetical order by last name. You can sort by state so that you can instantly see the names of all your customers who live in South Carolina.

Why You Need This Book

All of Works' features will make working with information easy. Using this program will save you time and make your work more efficient. But learning to use the many features is difficult at first. That's why you need this book.

This book is designed to make learning Works *easy*. This book helps the beginning Works user perform basic operations. Following the step-by-step instructions, you can learn how to take advantage of the many options in the program.

You don't have to worry that you don't know enough about computers or about Works to use the program. This book will teach you all that you need to know.

You don't have to worry that you might do something wrong and ruin a document or the computer. This book will point out mistakes you might make and show you how to avoid them. This book will explain how to change your mind—how to escape from a situation.

Reading this book will build your confidence. You can learn what tasks you need to perform to get a particular job done.

How This Book Is Organized

This book is designed with you, the beginner, in mind. The book is divided into several parts:

- Introduction
- The Basics
- Task/Review
- Reference

The Introduction explains how the book is set up and how to use the book.

The next part, The Basics, outlines general information about your computer and its keyboard layout. This part explains basic concepts, such as defining the tools, selecting commands, and understanding the document window.

The main portion of this book, the Task/Review part, tells you how to perform a particular task. The first task tells you how to start the program.

The last part, Reference, contains a quick reference of the most commonly used features, a keyboard guide, and a glossary. The glossary contains definitions of computer terms and explanations of those terms that apply to Works.

How To Use This Book

This book is set up so that you can use it several different ways:

- You can read the book from start to finish.
- You can start reading at any point in the book.
- You can experiment with one exercise, many exercises, or all exercises.
- You can look up specific tasks that you want to accomplish, such as making text bold.
- You can flip through the book, looking at the Before and After screens, to find specific tasks.
- You can look through the alphabetical list of tasks at the beginning of the Task/Review part to find the task you want.
- You can read just the exercise, just the review, or both the exercise and review sections. As you learn the program, you might want to follow along with the exercises. After you learn the program, you can use the review section to remind yourself how to perform a certain task.
- You can read any part of the exercises you want. You can read all the text to see both the steps to follow and the explanation of the steps. You can read only the text in red to see the commands to select and keystrokes to press. You can read just the explanation to understand what happens during a particular step.

Task section

The Task section includes numbered steps that tell you how to accomplish certain tasks, such as making text bold. The numbered steps walk you through a specific example so that you can learn the task by doing it. Blue text below the numbered steps explains the concept in more detail.

Oops! notes

You may find that you performed a task that you do not want after all. The Oops! notes tell you how to undo each procedure or explain how to get out of a situation. By showing you how to reverse nearly every procedure, these notes enable you to use Works more confidently.

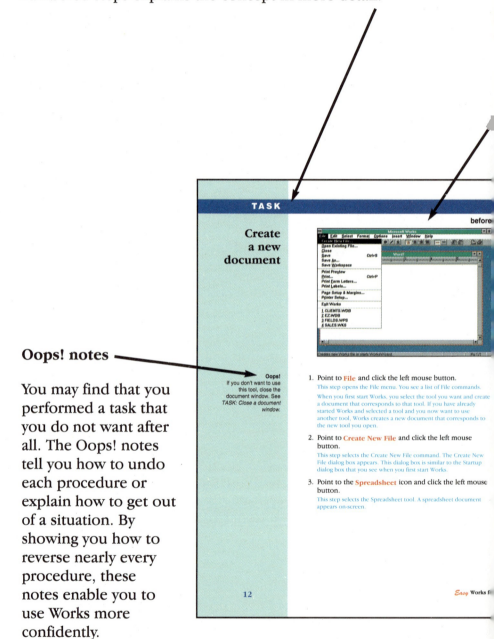

Before and After Screens

Each task includes Before and After screens that show how the computer screen will look before and after you follow the numbered steps in the Task section.

Review section

After you learn a procedure by following a specific example, you can refer to the Review section for a quick summary of the task. The Review section gives you generic steps for completing a task so that you can apply them to your own work. You can use these steps as a quick reference to refresh your memory about how to perform procedures.

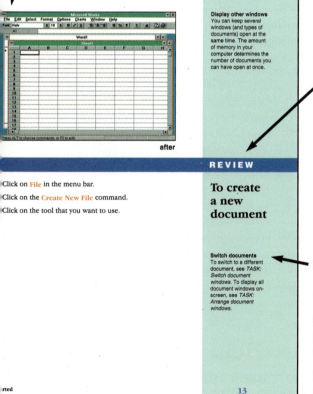

Other notes

The extra margin notes explain a little more about each procedure. These notes define terms, explain other options, and refer you to other sections, when applicable.

Introduction

How To Follow an Exercise

Works is flexible because it allows you to perform a task in many different ways. For consistency, this book makes certain assumptions about how your computer is set up and how you use Works. As you follow along with each exercise, keep the following key points in mind:

- This book assumes that you followed the basic installation. This book assumes that you have installed a printer and that you have not changed any program defaults. (For further explanations of your system, see *Understanding Your Computer System* in the Basics part.)

- This book assumes that you use the mouse to select data, to move the insertion point or cell pointer, and to select menu commands. Remember that you can also use the keyboard to accomplish these tasks.

- In the task sections, this book assumes that you are starting from the Before screen. If this screen contains any text or data, you should type what appears in this screen.

- Only the Before and After screens are illustrated. Screens are not shown for every step within an exercise. Where necessary, the text discusses screen messages and how to respond to them.

- This book covers only the word processing, spreadsheet, and database tools of Works. For information on using the other modules—draw and charts—and on integrating the data, see Que's *Using Microsoft Works for Windows*.

Where To Get More Help

This book does not cover all Works features or all ways of completing a task. This book is geared toward the beginning user—someone who wants just the basics. This person isn't ready for advanced features such as importing a graphic or creating a database report. This book covers just the most common, basic features.

As you become more comfortable, you may need a more complete reference book. You might be interested in *Using Microsoft Works for Windows* (published by Que).

You also might find the following Que titles helpful:

Using Windows 3.1, Special Edition

Easy Windows, 3.1 Edition

Que's *Computer User's Dictionary,* 3rd Edition

Introduction to Personal Computers, 3rd Edition

The Basics

Understanding Your Computer System

Using a Mouse

Using Your Keyboard

Understanding the Tools

Understanding the Document Window

Working with Windows

Selecting a Menu Command

Moving the Insertion Point

Saving and Retrieving Your Work

Easy **Works for Windows**

The Basics

Understanding Your Computer System

Think of your computer as just another appliance. Even though each model is different, they all have similar parts. After you learn how to use a washer or dryer, you could probably figure out how to use any washer or dryer. Similarly, after you start using a computer, you should be able to figure out how to use any computer.

Your computer system is made up of these basic parts:

- The system unit
- The monitor
- The keyboard
- The floppy disk drive(s)
- The hard disk drive

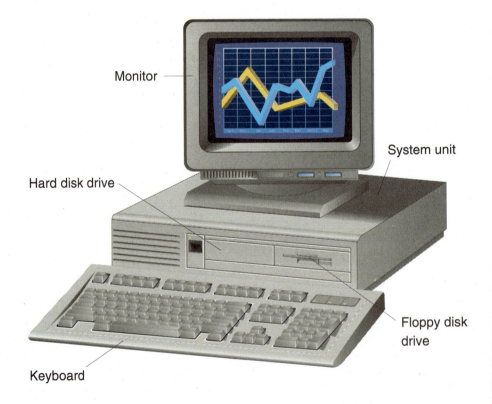

You probably also have a mouse and a printer.

System Unit. The system unit is the box that holds the electrical components of your computer. (The size of the system unit varies.) Somewhere on this box, you will find a power switch. The location and name of this switch—I/O, Power, and so on—varies. Check your computer manual.

Monitor. The monitor displays on-screen what you type on the keyboard. Your monitor might have a separate power switch. Turn on this switch, also.

Keyboard. The keyboard enables you to communicate with the computer. You use it to type entries and to issue commands. You type on the keyboard just as you do on a regular typewriter. A keyboard also has special keys that you use. (Different computers have different keyboards.) These keys are discussed in the section *Using Your Keyboard*.

Floppy Disk Drive. The floppy disk drive is the door into your computer. It allows you to put information onto the computer—onto the hard drive—and to take information off the computer—onto a floppy disk.

Hard Disk Drive. A hard disk drive stores the programs and files with which you work. To use Works, you must have a hard disk drive.

Printer. The printer lets you print the documents that you create. You must attach and install a printer if you intend to create paper copies of your on-screen documents. You install the printer through Windows. For information, see your Windows manual or *Using Windows 3.1,* Special Edition.

Mouse. The mouse, a pointing device, enables you to move the insertion point, choose menu options, and select text.

Using a Mouse

Using the mouse is the easiest and most natural way to learn Works and other Windows programs. This book assumes that you are using a mouse. (For information about using the keyboard, check the *Keyboard Guide* in the Reference section of this book.)

When you move the mouse on the desk, the mouse pointer moves on-screen. You can use the mouse to

- Select menu commands (see *Selecting a Menu Command* later in this part)
- Select information (text, cells, or fields)

There are four types of mouse actions:

Action	Procedure
Point	Place the mouse pointer on an item. Be sure that you place the tip of the pointer on the object.
Click	Point to an item, press the left mouse button, and release the mouse button.
Double-click	Point to an item and press the left mouse button twice in rapid succession.
Drag	Point to an item. Press and hold down the left mouse button, and then move the mouse. After the item you are dragging is where you want it, release the mouse button.

Keep these terms in mind as you follow the tasks in this book.

If you double-click the mouse and nothing happens, you might not have clicked quickly enough. Try again.

Using Your Keyboard

A computer keyboard is just like a typewriter, only a keyboard has these additional keys:

- Function keys such as F1
- Modifier keys
- Arrow keys
- Editing keys such as Del and Insert

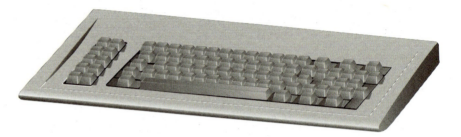

Original PC keyboard

AT keyboard

Enhanced keyboard

These keys are located in different places on different keyboards. On some keyboards, for example, the function keys are across the top of the keyboard. On other keyboards, the function keys are on the left side of the keyboard.

Your keyboard has most if not all the same keys as other keyboards, although the keys might be located in a different place. You can familiarize yourself with the keyboard by reading the names on the keys.

The Function Keys

For some commands, Works provides a function key shortcut. Rather than use the menu, you can press a function key to access the command. To select the Help command, for example, you can press the F1 key.

Shortcut Keys

For some commands, you use a *key combination*—a letter or number key and a modifier key. The Shift key is an example of a modifier key. You're probably familiar with the Shift key from a typewriter. You press Shift and t, for instance, to create a different letter—uppercase T. The Alt and Ctrl keys are special modifier keys. They work just like Shift. For instance, press and hold down the Ctrl key and then press B (specified as Ctrl+B) to select the Bold command. Press and hold down the Alt key and then press the Backspace key (Alt+Backspace) to select the Edit Undo command.

To press any key, just tap it once. (Some keys will repeat if you hold them down too long.) To use a key combination, press and hold down the first key; then press the second key. Key combinations in this book are indicated with a plus sign.

Keyboard shortcuts are listed on the Works menu. Also, this book covers some shortcuts in the exercises and in the quick reference guide.

Arrow Keys

You use the arrow keys to move around on-screen. There are also other movement keys such as PgUp, Home, End, and PgDn. These keys are also used to move the insertion point. For more information, see the section *Moving the Insertion Point*.

Your keyboard might have two sets of arrow keys and editing keys (Delete and Insert)—one set to the right of the alphanumeric keys and another set on the numeric keypad. You can use either set; the effect is the same.

Other Special Keys

Here's a short list of other special keys:

Key	Function
Backspace	Deletes the character to the left of the insertion point
Delete	Deletes the character to the right of the insertion point.
Esc	Enables you to back out of situations—close a menu without making a selection, close a dialog box, or cancel a change in the formula bar.

Understanding the Tools

Works is made up of several different tools:

Tool	Function
Word processor tool	Enables you to create letters, memos, form letters, and other documents. This tool works mainly with words.
Spreadsheet tool	Lets you create financial documents: budgets, forecasts, income statements, and so on. This tool works mainly with numbers.

continues

Tool	Function
Database tool	Enables you to store lists of items, people, or events: personnel records, client lists, inventory lists, invoice activity, and so on. This tool works on data in a set format.
Chart tool	Works with the spreadsheet tool so that you can create a graphic representation of your data. This book does not cover the Chart tool.
Draw tool	Lets you create logos, diagrams, and pictures. You can insert these drawings into documents created with the word processor. This book does not cover the Draw tool.

When you first start Works, you must select the type of tool with which you want to work:

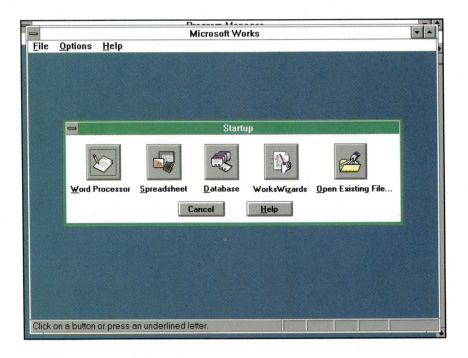

When you select the tool, Works creates the appropriate document type and opens the document window.

Understanding the Document Window

The document window that appears on-screen depends on the tool you are using.

Here is the document window for the word processor tool:

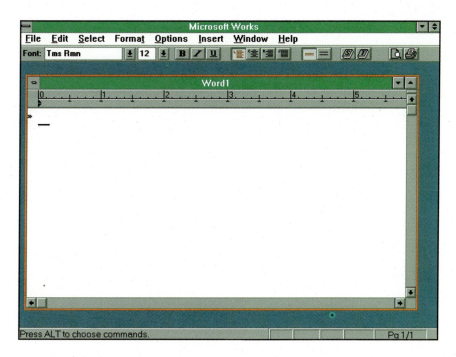

Here is the document window for the spreadsheet tool:

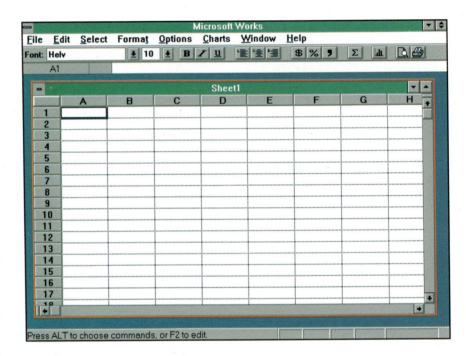

Here is the document window for the database tool:

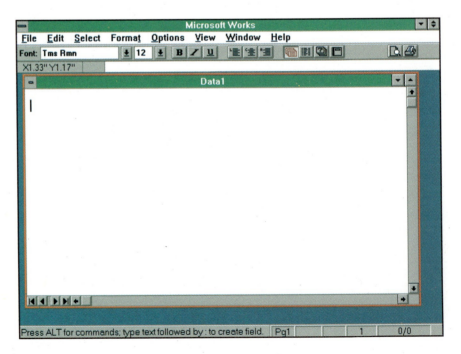

The default name appears in the title bar at the top of the document window. You can tell the type of window by the default name:

Name	Document type
Word1	Word processing document
Sheet1	Spreadsheet document
Data1	Database document

Each window has unique features, but they also have some elements in common. Here are some important areas of the screen:

- Application title bar
- Menu bar
- Toolbar
- Workspace
- Document title bar
- Status bar
- Scroll bar

The title bar at the top of the screen displays the name of the application.

The menu bar is located under the title bar. This line displays the main menu names. The menu names will vary depending on the tool you are using. To select a menu command, see the section *Selecting a Menu Command*.

The Toolbar displays buttons that allow you to access frequently used commands. For instance, click on the button with B to access the Bold command. The Toolbar is covered in the Quick Reference section of the Reference part.

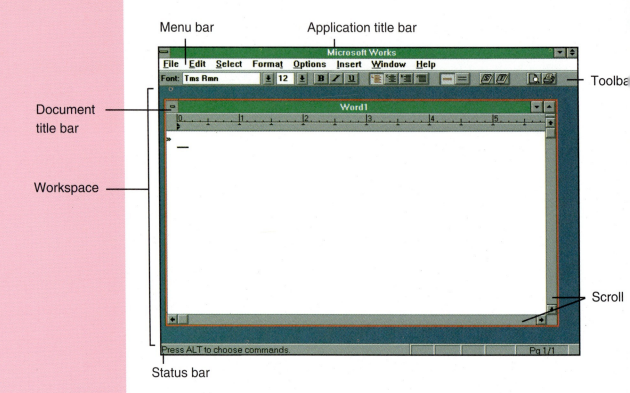

Below the Toolbar is the workspace area. Within this area, you can open document windows. You can have more than one document window (and type) open at the same time. Each window has a title bar that displays the name of the document. If you haven't saved (and named) the document, a default name—such as Data1—appears in the title bar.

The status bar appears at the bottom of the screen. This line displays messages, information about the location of the insertion point, and other information.

Working with Windows

Documents in Works appear in *windows* on-screen. You can do the following:

- Close the window
- Move and resize the window
- Maximize the window
- Scroll the window

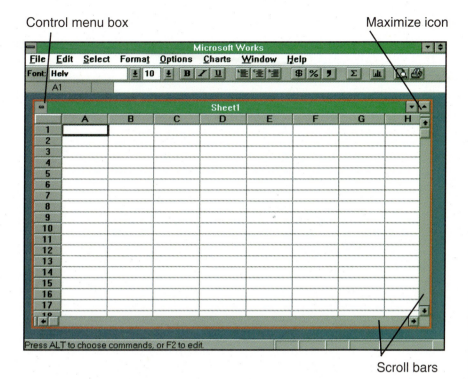

If you're already familiar with Microsoft Windows, you probably know how to perform these tasks. This section covers some basic Microsoft Windows techniques. For complete information, see *Using Windows 3.1,* Special Edition, or *Easy Windows,* 3.1 Edition.

Most windows have a Control menu box in the upper left corner in the title bar. Clicking on this menu box opens the Control menu and displays the available commands. You use this menu to manipulate the window (resize, maximize, close, and so on). Click on the command you want.

Closing the Window

To close the window, double-click the Control menu box. If you haven't saved your document, you will be prompted to do so. You can save and then close the document, or just abandon it.

Moving and Resizing the Window

To move a window, click on the title bar and hold down the mouse button. Then drag the window to the new location. When the window is in place, release the mouse button.

To resize a window, move the mouse pointer over the border of the side that you want to change. When the mouse pointer is the proper position, the pointer changes to a two-headed arrow. Click and hold down the mouse button; then drag the side until the window is the size you want. Release the mouse button.

Maximizing the Window

The title bar contains a Maximize icon (an up arrow). Click on the Maximize icon to expand the window so that it covers the entire screen.

Scrolling the Window

Scroll bars appear at the bottom and the right edge of a window. The majority of the scroll bar is shaded. Inside the scroll bar is a scroll box that indicates the relative position of the window display. If the scroll box is located in the center of the scroll bar, you are viewing the middle portion of a document. At the ends of the bars are scroll arrows.

You can use these two methods to scroll the window:

- Click on the scroll arrow to scroll the window in the direction of the arrow one line at a time.

- Drag the scroll box to move the relative distance in the direction that you are dragging.

Selecting a Menu Command

You access commands through Works' menu system. Click on the menu that you want to open; for example, click on File. A list of commands appears, as in the following screen:

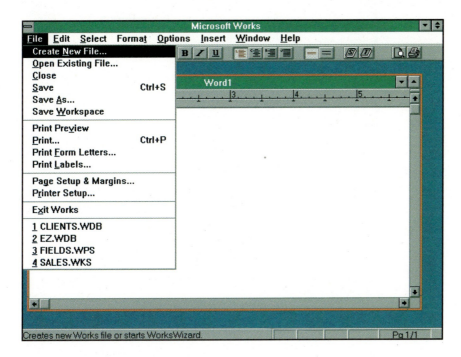

To select a command, click on that command.

If you display a menu that you don't want, press the Esc key. The menu closes.

When a command is followed by an ellipsis (...), you must specify additional options before you initiate the command. In this case, a *dialog box* appears. A dialog box enables you to select the additional options; you may need to type text, choose a selection, or confirm the operation. When you select the File Open Existing File command, for example, the Open dialog box appears:

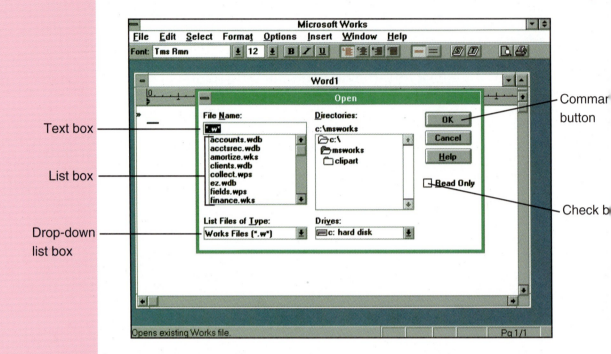

Dialog boxes can contain different elements. Each item may require a different type of selection process. Here are some of the most common elements:

Element	Description
Text box	A box within a dialog box in which you type information—such as a file name. To select a text box, click in the box. (Sometimes the insertion point is already positioned in the text box.)
Check box	A square box that appears in a dialog box. Check boxes can be checked (selected) or unchecked (unselected). To select a check box, click in the box. To unselect a check box, click in that box again.

Element	Description
List box	A list of available choices—such as file names or directories. To select an item in a list, click on it. Sometimes list boxes have scroll bars that you can use to scroll through the list by clicking on the down scroll arrow or up scroll arrow.
Drop-down list box	A list box that displays only the first item in the list. To display other items, click on the down arrow in the drop-down list.
Option button	A round button that appears in a dialog box. To select an option, click in the option button. A dot appears in the button. You cannot activate more than one option button at a time in that particular dialog box. Some dialog boxes have more than one group of option buttons.
Command button	A choice of action that is displayed in a dialog box. Two common command buttons are OK and Cancel. To select a command button, click on it. Most dialog boxes have a "default" command or option button. To select the default button, you can either click on the button or just press Enter.

You can also use the keyboard to select menu commands. See the *Keyboard Guide* in the Reference part of this book.

Moving the Insertion Point

To use the mouse to move the insertion point, move the mouse pointer on-screen and click where you want to position the insertion point.

You can use the arrow keys and other key combinations to move the insertion point. Here is a list of the most common keys:

To move	**Press**
One character or cell right	→
One character or cell left	←
One line or row up	↑
One line or row down	↓
Beginning of document	Ctrl+Home
End of document	Ctrl+End

Saving and Retrieving Your Work

Your work is stored temporarily in memory, much like if you have a shopping list in your head. Until you commit the list to paper, you might forget some or all of the items. The same is true with Works. Until you save the document, you can lose all or part of your work.

Saving the document doesn't commit it to paper like the shopping list. Saving the document saves the document to your disk. Then when you need the document again, you can retrieve it from the disk.

Works does not automatically save your work. You should save every 5 or 10 minutes. If you don't save your work, you could lose it. Suppose that you have been working on a document for a few hours. Then the electricity is turned off unexpectedly because an air conditioning repairman at your office shorts out the power or a thunderstorm hits—any number of things can cause a power loss. If the power goes off, you will lose all your hard work if you haven't saved.

The word processor, spreadsheet, and database sections describe how to save a file.

Task/Review

Getting Started

Word Processor

Spreadsheet

Database

Easy **Works for Windows**

Alphabetical Listing of Tasks

Add a field 178
Add a label 174
Add a record in form view 194
Add a record in list view 208
Align text 148
Arrange document windows 52
Boldface text 82
Center text 92
Change the field width 206
Change the font 88
Change the font size 90
Change the size of a field 184
Change to list view 204
Check spelling 96
Clear a range 140
Close a document window 54
Combine paragraphs 68
Copy a cell entry 132
Copy a formula 144
Copy a range 138
Copy text 76
Create a database 172
Create a document 60
Create a new document 48
Create a spreadsheet 116
Delete a column 156
Delete a field 186
Delete a record in form view 202
Delete a record in list view 212
Delete a row 160
Delete text 74

Display a record in form view 196
Edit a cell entry 128
Edit a field name 180
Edit a record in form view 198
Edit a record in list view 210
Enter a date 122
Enter a field name 176
Enter a formula 124
Enter a number 120
Enter a page break 70
Enter a record in form view 192
Enter text 118
Erase a cell entry 130
Exit Works for Windows 56
Find a record in form view 200
Format a range 150
Get help 46
Indent text 94
Insert a blank line 66
Insert a column 154
Insert a row 158
Insert text 64
Italicize text 84
Make an entry bold 152
Move a cell entry 134
Move a field 182
Move a range 142
Move text 78
Open a database 190
Open a document 108
Open a spreadsheet 164

39

Preview a database 216
Preview a document 110
Preview a spreadsheet 166
Print a database 218
Print a document 112
Print a spreadsheet 168
Replace text 102
Save a database 188
Save a document 106
Save a spreadsheet 162
Search for text 100
Select a range 136
Select a tool 44
Select text 72
Set column width 146
Sort records 214
Start Works for Windows 42
Switch document windows 50
Type text 62
Underline text 86
Use a function 126
Use Undo 80

Getting Started

This section includes the following tasks:

Start Works for Windows

Select a tool

Get help

Create a new document

Switch document windows

Arrange document windows

Close a document window

Exit Works for Windows

TASK

Start Works for Windows

before

Oops!
Be sure that you double-click the mouse. If you click twice and nothing happens or if the icon slides around, you might have waited too long between clicks. Try double-clicking again.

1. Turn on the computer and monitor.

   Every computer has a different location for its power switch. Check the side, the front, and the back of your computer. Your monitor also might have a separate power switch; if so, you need to turn on this power switch also.

2. If necessary, respond to the prompts for date and time.

   Some systems ask you to enter the current date and time. (Many of the newer models enter the time and date automatically. If you aren't prompted for these entries, don't worry.)

   If you are prompted, type the current date and press Enter. Then type the current time and press Enter.

3. Type **win** and press **Enter**.

   Win is the command to start Microsoft Windows. You see the Program Manager on-screen. The Program Manager is an application that comes with Microsoft Windows.

4. Double-click on the group icon for **Microsoft SolutionSeries**.

   To double-click, click the mouse button twice in rapid succession. This step opens the Works for Windows program group. This program group is probably called Microsoft SolutionSeries. In Microsoft Windows, programs are stored in group windows.

   If the window is already open, you can skip this step.

42

Easy **Works for Windows**

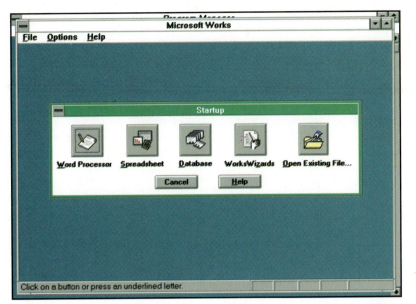

after

5. Double-click on the program icon for **Microsoft Works**.

   This step starts the Works for Windows program. You see the Startup dialog box. This dialog box enables you to select a tool (word processor, spreadsheet, database, or WorksWizard) or open an existing document. (See *TASK: Select a tool*.)

Exit Works
To exit Works, see *TASK: Exit Works for Windows*.

REVIEW

To start Works for Windows

1. Turn on your computer and monitor.
2. Respond to the prompts for the date and time, if necessary.
3. Type **win** and press **Enter**.
4. Double-click on the group icon for **Microsoft SolutionSeries**.
5. Double-click on the program icon for **Microsoft Works**.

Install the program
To start Works for Windows, the program must be installed. Follow the installation procedures outlined in the Works for Windows manual.

Getting Started

43

TASK

Select a tool

before

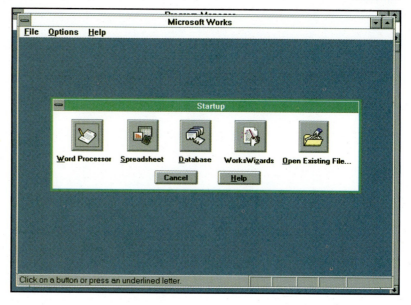

Oops!
If you have already started Works and want to switch tools, see *TASK: Create a new document*.

With the Startup dialog box on-screen, point to **Word Processor** and click the left mouse button.

This step selects the word processor tool. You see a blank document window on-screen. The word processor is covered in the next section of this book.

Each time you start Works, the Startup dialog box appears on-screen. If you have already started the program and want to create a new document, see *TASK: Create a new document*.

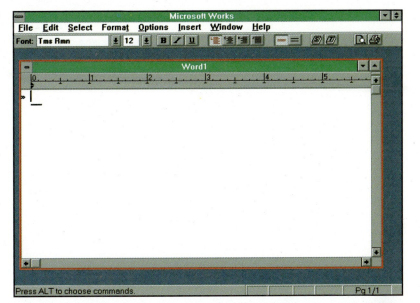

after

With the Startup dialog box on-screen, click on the tool you want.

Close the document window
If you want to close the document window, see *TASK: Close a document window*.

REVIEW

To select a tool

Getting Started

45

TASK

Get help

before

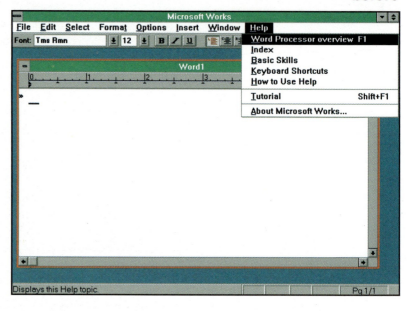

Oops!
Double-click on the Control menu box to close the Help window.

1. Point to **Help** and click the left mouse button.

   The Help menu is located in the menu bar. This step opens the Help menu. On-screen you see a list of Help menu options.

   Each module has a Help menu. The commands listed might vary, depending on the tool that is open.

2. Point to **Index** and click the left mouse button.

   This step chooses the Index command. The Help window opens and you see a list of topics.

3. Point to **Word Processor** and click the left mouse button.

   This step displays additional topics. Be sure to click on the word—not the icon. When the mouse pointer is positioned on a topic for which you can get help, the pointer changes to a hand with a pointing finger.

4. Point to **Word Processor basics** and click the left mouse button.

   This step displays subtopics for the selected topic.

5. Point to **Creating a Word Processing document** and click the left mouse button.

   This step displays help on the selected topic. You see an explanation of how to create a document. You can scroll this window by clicking on the scroll arrows. When you have read the explanation, close the Help window by following steps 6 and 7.

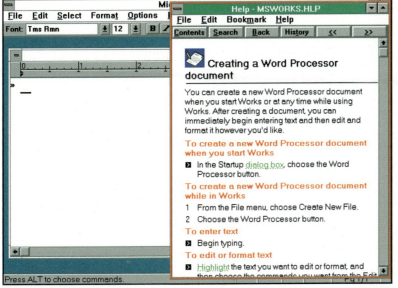

after

6. Point to **File** and click the left mouse button.
   This step opens the File menu. Be sure to click on the File menu within the Help window.

7. Point to **Exit** and click the left mouse button.
   This step selects the Exit command and closes the Help window.

REVIEW

To get help

1. Click on **Help** in the menu bar.
2. Click on the **Index** command.
3. Click on the topic you want.
4. Click on the subtopic you want.
5. Click on the next subtopic you want.
6. To close Help, click on **File** in the menu bar.
7. Click on the **Exit** command.

More help?
Works offers many ways to get help, and the Help feature has its own menu system. For complete information on all Help options, see *Using Works for Windows*.

Help on all tools
No matter which tool you are using, you can still get help on any of the other tools.

TASK

Create a new document

before

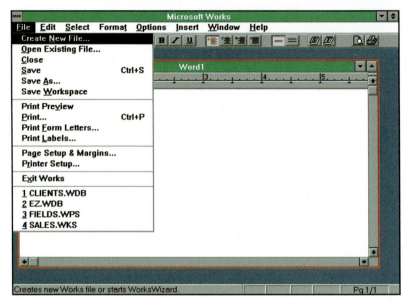

Oops!
If you don't want to use the spreadsheet tool, close the document window. See *TASK: Close a document window*.

1. Point to **File** and click the left mouse button.

   This step opens the File menu. You see a list of File commands.

   When you start Works, you select the tool you want and create a document that corresponds to that tool. If you have already started Works and selected a tool and you now want to use another tool, Works creates a new document that corresponds to the new tool you open.

2. Point to **Create New File** and click the left mouse button.

   This step selects the Create New File command. The Create New File dialog box appears. This dialog box is similar to the Startup dialog box that you see when you first start Works.

3. Point to the **Spreadsheet** icon and click the left mouse button.

   This step selects the spreadsheet tool. A spreadsheet document appears on-screen.

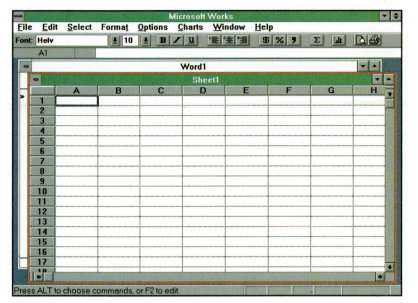

after

1. Click on **File** in the menu bar.
2. Click on the **Create New File** command.
3. Click on the tool that you want to use.

Display other windows
You can keep several windows (and types of documents) open at the same time. The amount of memory in your computer determines the number of documents you can have open at once.

REVIEW

To create a new document

Switch documents
To switch to a different document, see *TASK: Switch document windows*. To display all document windows on-screen, see *TASK: Arrange document windows*.

Getting Started

49

TASK

Switch document windows

before

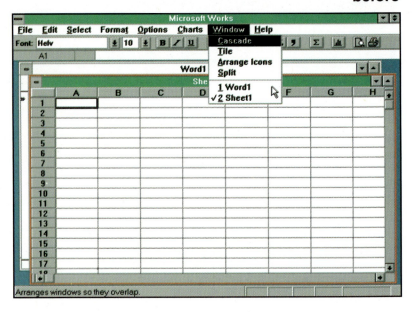

Oops!
Follow this same procedure to make another window active.

1. **Point to Window and click the left mouse button.**

   This step opens the Window menu and displays a list of Window commands. At the bottom of the menu, you see a list of the windows that are open. A check mark appears next to the current window. (If you have named and saved the files, the file names appear. If you haven't named and saved the files, the default file names appear.)

   The Before screen shows two open windows: a word processing window (Word1) and a spreadsheet window (Sheet1). For help creating these documents, see *TASK: Create a new document*.

2. **Point to Word1 and click the left mouse button.**

   This step selects the word processing window and makes it the active window. You can tell which window is active—that is, which window you can type in—by looking at the title bar. The active window has a darker or colored title bar.

   Also, the menus in the menu bar are different, depending on what type of window is active.

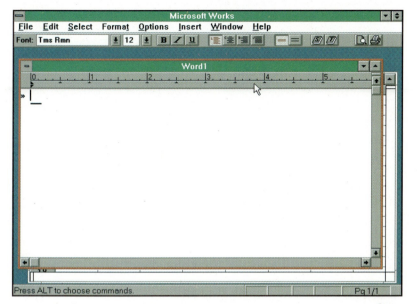

after

1. Click on **Window** in the menu bar.

2. Click on the window name that you want to make active.

REVIEW

To switch document windows

Try a shortcut
If you can see the window that you want to make active, you can click on it. The window will become active.

Arrange windows
You can arrange the windows so that you can see them all on-screen. See *TASK: Arrange document windows*.

TASK

Arrange document windows

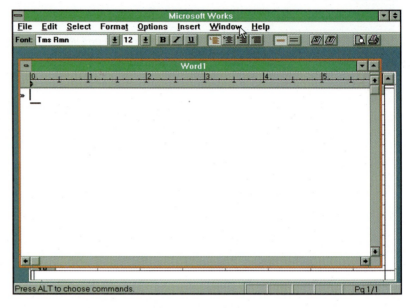

before

Oops!
To restore a window to a full-screen display, make it the active window and then click on the Maximize icon (the up arrow in the document window's title bar).

1. **Point to Window and click the left mouse button.**

   This step opens the Window menu and displays a list of Window commands.

   In this task, two windows are open: a word processing window (Word1) and a spreadsheet window (Sheet1). You only see Word1, however.

2. **Point to Tile and click the left mouse button.**

   This step selects the Tile command. All the open windows are arranged on-screen. Notice that the active window has a darker or differently colored title bar from the nonactive window.

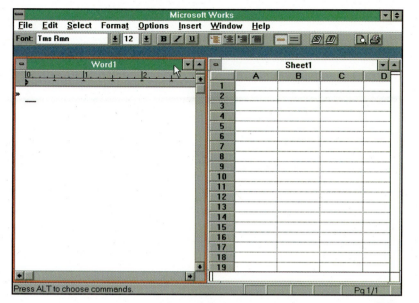
after

1. Click on **Window** in the menu bar.
2. Click on the **Tile** command.

Close a window
To close a window, see
TASK: Close a document window.

REVIEW

To arrange document windows

See different menus?
Depending on which window is active, you will see a different set of menus. Remember that each tool has different commands and that the active window corresponds to the tool. That is, if you are working in a spreadsheet window, you will see commands that correspond to the spreadsheet tool.

Getting Started

TASK

Close a document window

Oops!
To open a document window, see *TASK: Create a new document*.

before

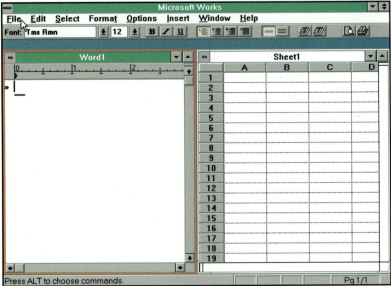

1. Point to **File** and click the left mouse button.

   This step opens the File menu. You see a list of File commands.

   For this task, the active window is the word processing window (Word1). If you want to close a different window, make that window active.

2. Click on **Close**.

   This step selects the Close command and closes the window. If you have typed information in the document, Works prompts you to save the document. See the tasks on saving in the word processing, spreadsheet, or database sections.

   If other document windows are open, they will remain open in the work area. If only one document window is open and you close it, you will see the menu bar and a blank work area (no document windows). You can then exit Works, create a new document, or open an existing document.

Easy **Works for Window**

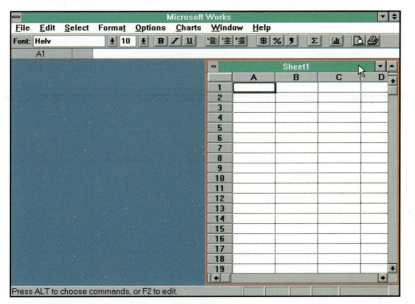

after

Why close a window?
If you select the wrong tool or decide to abandon a document, simply close the window.

1. Click on **File** in the menu bar.
2. Click on the **Close** command.

REVIEW

To close a document window

Getting Started

55

TASK

Exit Works for Windows

Oops!
To restart Works for Windows, see *TASK: Start Works for Windows*.

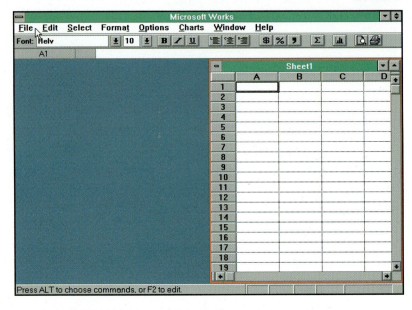

before

1. Point to **File** and click the left mouse button.
   This step opens the File menu. You see a list of File commands.

2. Point to **Exit Works** and click the left mouse button.
   This step chooses the Exit Works command. You return to the Windows Program Manager.

   To exit Windows and return to DOS, follow steps 3 through 5.

3. In the Program Manager, point to **File** and click the left mouse button.
   This step opens the File menu. You see a list of File commands.

4. Point to **Exit Windows** and click the left mouse button.
   This step selects the Exit Windows command. On-screen you see the Exit Windows dialog box.

5. Point to **OK** and click the left mouse button.
   This step confirms that you do want to exit. You return to DOS; the prompt C:\> appears on-screen.

after

Save a document
If you have typed any text or made any unsaved changes to the document, Works prompts you to save the changes. See the tasks on saving a document.

REVIEW

To exit Works for Windows

1. Click on **File** in the menu bar.
2. Click on the **Exit** command.

   To exit Windows, follow steps 3 through 5.

3. Click on **File** in the menu bar.
4. Click on the **Exit Windows** command.
5. Click on the **OK** button or press **Enter**.

Try a shortcut
Press the Alt+F4 key combination to select the File Exit command.

Getting Started

Word Processing

This section includes the following tasks:

Create a document	Underline text
Type text	Change the font
Insert text	Change the font size
Insert a blank line	Center text
Combine paragraphs	Indent text
Enter a page break	Check spelling
Select text	Search for text
Delete text	Replace text
Copy text	Save a document
Move text	Open a document
Use Undo	Preview a document
Boldface text	Print a document
Italicize text	

TASK

Create a document

before

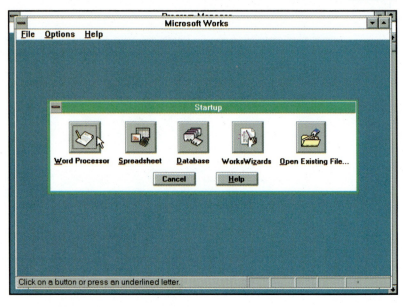

Oops!
If you don't want to create a document, close the document window. See *TASK: Close a document window.*

1. **Start Works for Windows.**

   For help with this step see *TASK: Start Works for Windows*. The Startup dialog box appears on-screen. The Before screen shows this step.

2. **Click on Word Processor.**

   This step selects the word processor tool and displays a blank word processing document in a window on-screen. Note two special areas of the word processing document window: the Toolbar and the Ruler.

   The Toolbar provides access to frequently used commands. To use an icon, click on it. For example, select text, and then click on the B icon to select the Bold command.

   The Ruler enables you to set tabs, change margins, and specify indents. For information on using the Ruler, see *Using Works for Windows*.

   The Toolbar and Ruler are displayed by default. You can choose to hide the Toolbar by selecting Show Toolbar from the Options menu. Select Show Ruler to hide the Ruler. When the Toolbar or Ruler is displayed, a check mark appears next to the menu option.

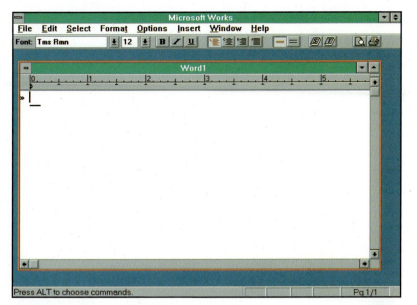

after

Works already started?
If you have already started Works and want to create a document, see *TASK: Create a new document*.

REVIEW

1. Start Works for Windows.
2. Click on the **Word Processor** tool.

To create a document

Word Processing

TASK

Type text

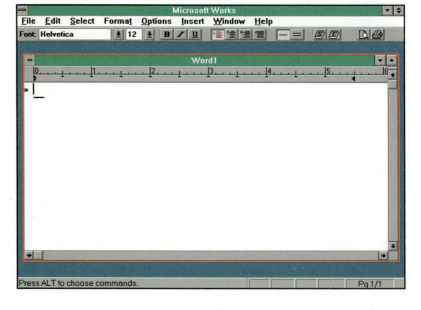

before

Oops!
Press the Backspace key to delete a character to the left of the insertion point.

Type the following:

New Listing! Come see this two bedroom doll house located in popular Broad Ripple. House has hardwood floors, built-in corner cabinet, and backyard.

When you type with a word processor, you can see the characters on-screen as you type. If you make a mistake, you can press the Backspace key to delete the previous character. Then you can type the correct character. When you reach the end of the line, you don't have to press Enter (or the Return key). Works moves the text to the next line automatically; this feature is called *word wrap*.

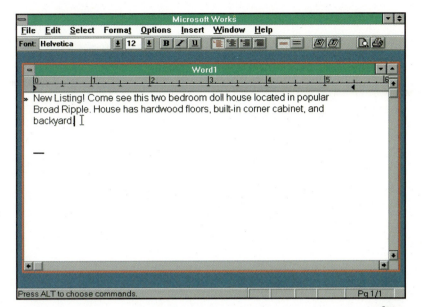

after

What is an insertion point?
The insertion point is a vertical line on-screen that indicates the place where text will be inserted if you start typing.

REVIEW

Type the text. Press **Enter** when you want to end a paragraph or insert a blank line.

To type text

Word Processing   63

TASK

Insert text

Oops!
To delete the text, select Edit Undo immediately after typing the new text. You also can simply delete the text; see *TASK: Delete text*.

before

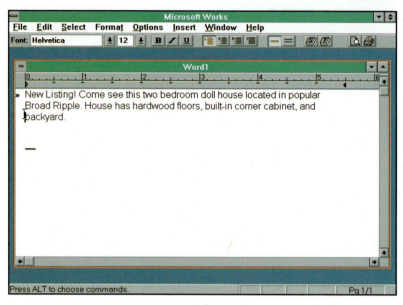

1. Click before the word *backyard*.

   This step places the insertion point where you want to insert text. You can place the insertion point by clicking the mouse button, or by pressing the arrow keys that point in the direction you want the insertion point to move.

   Remember to type any text that appears in the Before screen before you begin this exercise.

2. Type **fabulous**.

   The new text is inserted at the insertion point and pushes the existing text right.

3. Press the **space bar**.

   This step inserts a space between the new text and the original text.

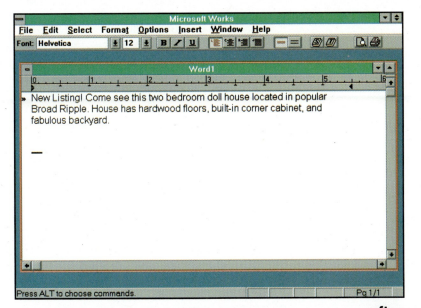
after

Overwrite text
You do not press the Insert key to insert text. Pressing this key places Works in Overtype mode. In this mode, characters that you type replace characters to the right of the insertion point; text does not move to make room for the new text.

REVIEW

1. Position the insertion point where you want to insert new text.
2. Type the text.
3. If necessary, insert a space.

To insert text

TASK

Insert a blank line

before

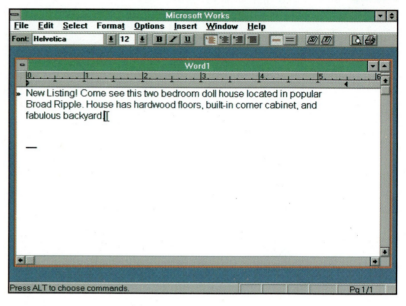

Oops!
To delete the blank line, see *TASK: Combine paragraphs.*

1. Click after the word *backyard*.

   Be sure to click after the period at the end of the sentence. This step places the insertion point where you want to insert a blank line.

   Remember to type any text that appears in the Before screen before you begin this exercise.

2. Press **Enter**.

   Pressing Enter ends the current paragraph.

3. Press **Enter**.

   Pressing Enter again inserts a blank line. When you press Enter, a paragraph mark is inserted into the document.

   By default, paragraph marks (¶) do not appear on-screen. If you want to display them so that you can see where paragraphs end, select Show All Characters from the Options menu. This option will also display tabs and spaces.

4. Type **Open house this Sunday.**

   This step enters a new line of text. Notice that a blank line separates the two paragraphs.

Easy **Works for Windows**

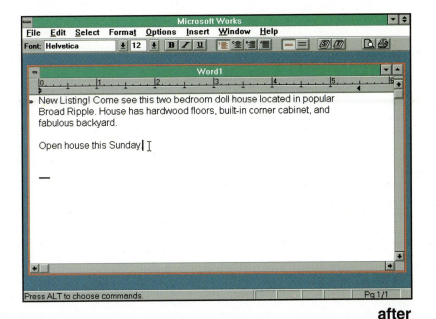
after

What is word wrap?
Unlike a typewriter, you don't have to press Enter at the end of each line of text. When text reaches the end of a line, Works automatically moves (wraps) additional text to the next line. You only need to press Enter at the end of a paragraph.

REVIEW

1. Move the insertion point to the end of the paragraph.
2. Press **Enter twice**.

To insert a blank line

Hard return vs. soft return
A *hard return* forces a line break. If you add or delete text, the hard return remains in the same place in the text. A *soft return* is inserted automatically by Works. When you add or delete text, the soft returns are adjusted.

Word Processing

67

TASK

Combine paragraphs

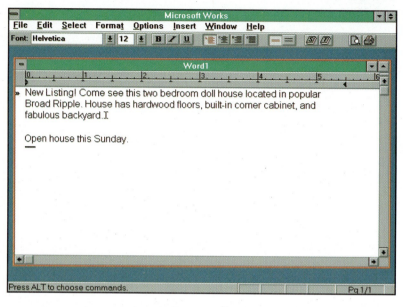

before

Oops!
To split the paragraphs, move the insertion point to where you want the break. Then press Enter. Press Enter twice if you want to insert a blank line between the paragraphs.

1. **Click after the word *backyard*.**

   Be sure to click after the period. This step places the insertion point at the end of the first paragraph.

   Remember to type any text that appears in the Before screen before you begin this exercise.

2. **Press Del.**

   Pressing the Del key deletes the paragraph marker at the end of the current paragraph.

3. **Press Del.**

   Pressing the Del key again deletes the blank line between the paragraphs. The second paragraph moves up next to the first paragraph.

4. **Press the space bar.**

   Pressing the space bar inserts a space between the two sentences.

Easy **Works for Windows**

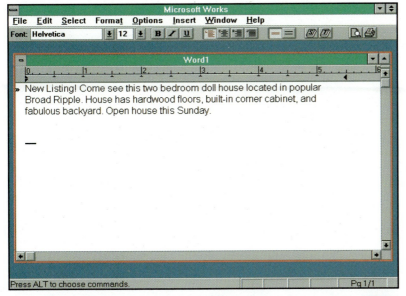

after

REVIEW

1. Move the insertion point to the end of the last line in the first paragraph.

2. Press **Del**. If there is a black line between the paragraphs, press **Del twice**.

3. Press the **space bar**.

To combine paragraphs

TASK

Enter a page break

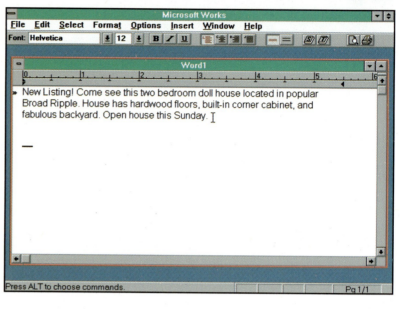

before

Oops!
To combine pages, select Edit Undo immediately after inserting the page break.

1. **Click after the word *Sunday*.**

   This step positions the insertion point where you want the new page to begin. Be sure to position the insertion point after the period, and remember that you can use the mouse or the arrow keys to position the insertion point.

   Remember to type any text that appears in the Before screen before you begin this exercise.

2. **Click on Insert.**

   This step opens the Insert menu. You see a list of Insert commands.

3. **Click on Page Break.**

   This step selects the Page Break command. A dotted line appears on-screen; this dotted line represents the page break. When you print the document, a new page will begin where you have inserted the page break.

   This page break is called a hard page break. A hard page break remains in place regardless of whether you add or delete text before it.

Easy **Works for Windows**

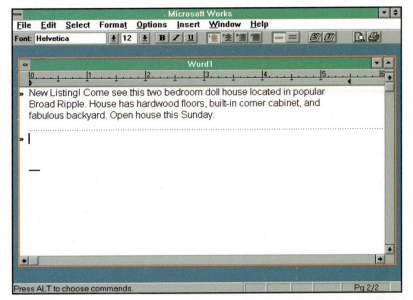
after

1. Position the insertion point where you want the new page to begin.
2. Click on **Insert** in the menu bar.
3. Click on the **Page Break** command.

Try a shortcut
Press the Ctrl+Enter key combination to enter a hard page break quickly.

REVIEW

To enter a page break

What is a soft page break?
When Works reaches the end of a page, it inserts a soft page break automatically. When you make changes to the document, Works repaginates the document and adjusts the location of the soft page breaks. A soft page break appears as a chevron («) in the left margin.

Word Processing

71

TASK

Select text

before

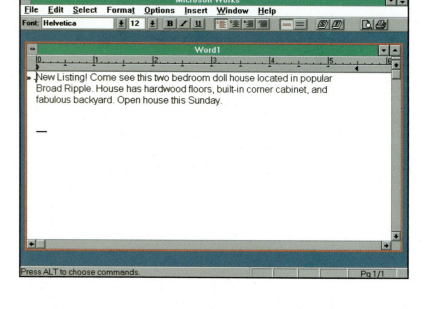

Oops!
To deselect text, click outside the selected text.

1. **Click before the *N* in *New Listing*.**

    This step places the insertion point where you want to start selecting text. You also can use the arrow keys to place the insertion point.

    Remember to type any text that appears in the Before screen before you begin this exercise.

2. **Hold down the mouse button and drag across the text until you highlight *New Listing!***

    This step selects the text. As long as you continue to hold down the mouse button, you can extend the selection.

3. **Release the mouse button.**

    The selected text appears in reverse video on-screen. (*Reverse video* means that the colors of the text and background are switched; you now see white text on a black background rather than black text on a white background.)

    After you select text, you can make many changes to it—delete it, copy it, move it, make it bold, and so on. See the other tasks in this section for more information.

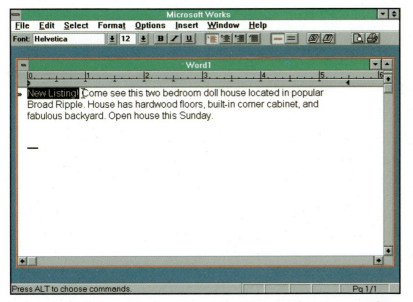

after

1. Click at the start of the text you want to select.
2. Hold down the mouse button and drag across the text you want to select.
3. Release the mouse button.

Use the keyboard
To select text by using the keyboard, position the insertion point where you want to start selecting. Then hold down the Shift key and use the arrow keys to highlight the text in the direction of the arrow key you are pressing.

REVIEW

To select text

Try some shortcuts
To select a word quickly, position the insertion point on the word and double-click the mouse button. To select a sentence quickly, position the insertion point on the sentence; then press and hold down the Ctrl key and click the mouse button. To select the entire document, select All from the Select menu.

Word Processing

TASK

Delete text

Oops!
To restore the deleted text, select Edit Undo.

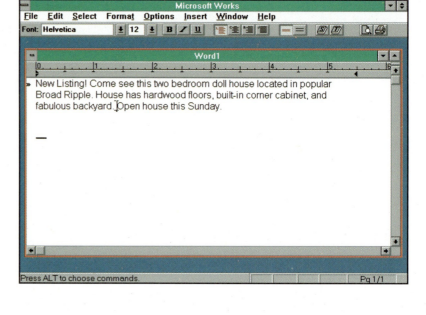

before

1. Click before the *O* in *Open house*.

   This step places the insertion point before the text you want to delete.

   Remember to type any text that appears in the Before screen before you begin this exercise.

2. Select the words *Open house this Sunday*.

   You can use either the mouse or the keyboard to select text. To use the mouse, hold down the mouse button, drag across the text that you want to select, and then release the mouse button. To use the keyboard, hold down the Shift key and use the arrow keys to select the text. (See *TASK: Select text* for more information.)

   Be sure to select the entire line, including the period at the end of the sentence.

3. Press **Del**.

   Pressing the Del key deletes the selected text. If there is text remaining to the right of the deleted text, the remaining text moves over to fill in the gap.

   You also can press the Backspace key to delete selected text.

Easy **Works for Window**

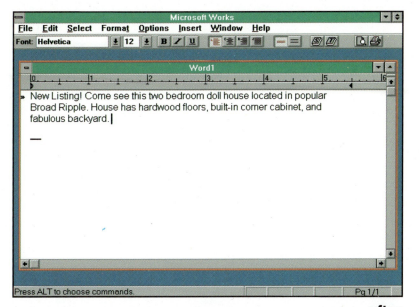

after

1. Select the text that you want to delete.
2. Press **Del** or **Backspace**.

Delete a character
To delete a single character, use the Delete or Backspace key. Press the Delete key to delete the character to the right of the insertion point; press the Backspace key to delete the character to the left of the insertion point.

REVIEW

To delete text

TASK

Copy text

before

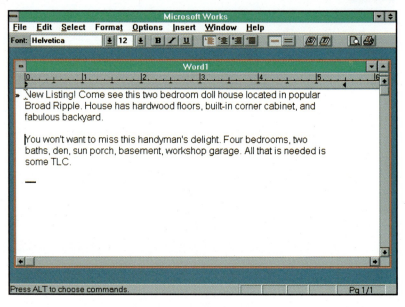

Oops!
To delete the copied text, select Edit Undo immediately after pasting the text. Or just delete the copied text.

1. Click before the *N* in *New Listing*.

   This step places the insertion point at the start of the text that you want to copy.

   Remember to type any text that appears in the Before screen before you begin this exercise.

2. Select the text *New Listing!*

   You can use either the mouse or the keyboard to select text. To use the mouse, hold down the mouse button, drag across the text that you want to select, and then release the mouse button. To use the keyboard, hold down the Shift key and use the arrow keys to select the text. See *TASK: Select text* for more information.

   Be sure to select the exclamation point and the space that follows the exclamation point.

3. Click on **Edit**.

   This step opens the Edit menu. You see a list of Edit commands.

4. Click on **Copy**.

   This step selects the Copy command. The text is copied to the Clipboard. The *Clipboard* is a temporary holding space for text and graphics.

Easy **Works for Window**

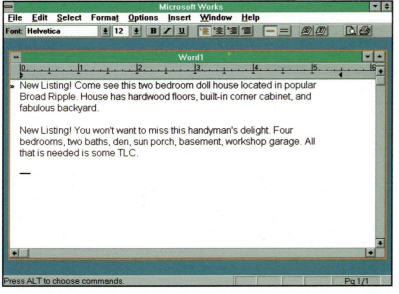

after

Try some shortcuts
Press the Ctrl+C key combination to select the Edit Copy command. Press the Ctrl+V key combination to select the Edit Paste command.

5. Click before the *Y* in *You* in the second paragraph.
   This step places the insertion point where you want the copied text to appear.

6. Click on **Edit**.
   This step opens the Edit menu again. You see a list of Edit commands.

7. Click on **Paste**.
   This step selects the Paste command. The copied text appears in both locations.

REVIEW

To copy text

1. Select the text that you want to copy.

2. Click on **Edit** in the menu bar.

3. Click on the **Copy** command.

4. Position the insertion point where you want to insert the copy.

5. Click on **Edit** in the menu bar.

6. Click on the **Paste** command.

Word Processing

77

TASK

Move text

before

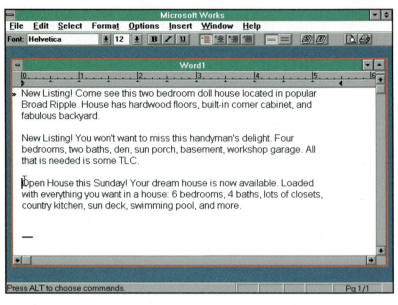

Oops!
To restore the text to the original location, select Edit Undo immediately after selecting Paste. Move the insertion point back to the original location and select Paste.

1. **Click the mouse before the *O* in *Open*.**

   This step places the insertion point at the start of the text that you want to move.

   Remember to type any text that appears in the Before screen before you begin this exercise.

2. **Select the entire paragraph.**

   You can use either the mouse or the keyboard to select text. To use the mouse, hold down the mouse button, drag across the text that you want to select, and then release the mouse button. To use the keyboard, hold down the Shift key and use the arrow keys to select the text. See *TASK: Select text* for more information.

3. **Click on Edit.**

   This step opens the Edit menu. You see a list of Edit commands.

4. **Click on Cut.**

   This step selects the Cut command. The text is cut from the document and placed on the Clipboard. The *Clipboard* is a temporary holding space for text and graphics.

5. **Click before the *N* in *New Listing* in the first paragraph.**

   This step positions the insertion point where you want to move the text.

6. **Click on Edit.**

   This step opens the Edit menu again. You see a list of Edit commands.

78

Easy **Works for Window**

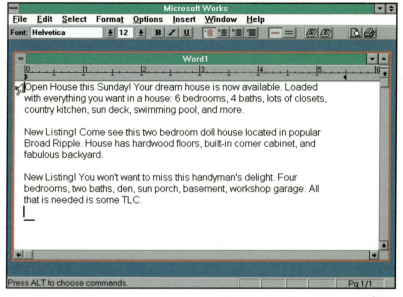
after

Try some shortcuts
Press the Ctrl+X key combination to select the Edit Cut command. Press the Ctrl+V key combination to select the Edit Paste command.

7. Click on **Paste**.
   This step selects the Paste command. The text is pasted into the document at the new location.

8. Insert a blank line between the first and second paragraphs.
   This step separates the two paragraphs. (For help with this step, see *TASK: Insert a blank line*.) Often when you move or copy, you will need to adjust the spacing (insert spaces or hard returns or delete spaces or hard returns).

REVIEW

To move text

1. Select the text that you want to move.
2. Click on **Edit** in the menu bar.
3. Click on the **Cut** command.
4. Position the insertion point where you want the text to appear.
5. Click on **Edit** in the menu bar.
6. Click on the **Paste** command.

TASK

Use Undo

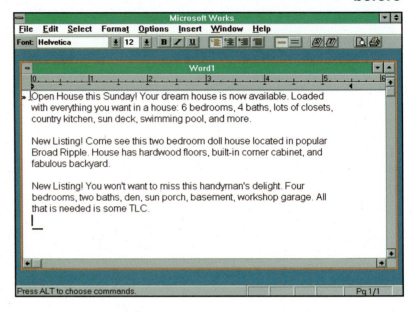

before

Oops!
Select Edit Undo again to undo the "undo."

1. **Click before the *O* in *Open* in the first paragraph.**

   This step places the insertion point at the start of the text you want to delete. In this task, you undo a text deletion.

   Remember to type any text that appears in the Before screen before you begin this exercise.

2. **Select the entire paragraph.**

   You can use either the mouse or the keyboard to select text. To use the mouse, hold down the mouse button, drag across the text that you want to select, and then release the mouse button. To use the keyboard, hold down the Shift key and use the arrow keys to select the text. See *TASK: Select text* for more information.

3. **Press Del.**

   Pressing the Del key deletes the selected text.

4. **Click on Edit.**

   This step opens the Edit menu. You see a list of Edit commands.

5. **Click on Undo.**

   This step selects the Undo command. The deleted text is restored; the text is still selected.

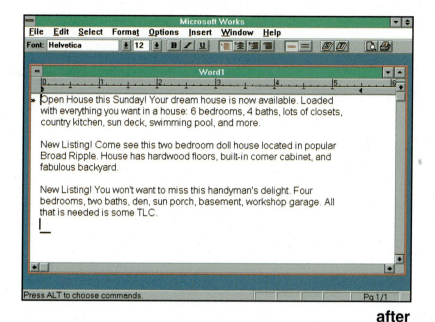

after

Try a shortcut
Press the Alt+Backspace key combination to select the Edit Undo command.

6. Click outside the text.

   This step deselects the text. Notice that the Before and After screens are the same.

   You can use Undo for other changes besides restoring deleted text. You can undo typing, editing, and formatting changes. You cannot undo merges, scrolling the document, selecting text, or any commands from the Options menu.

Select Undo immediately
Undo reverses only the *last* change you made to the document. If you make a change you want to undo, select Edit Undo immediately.

REVIEW

To use Undo

1. Click on **Edit** in the menu bar.
2. Click on the **Undo** command.

Word Processing

81

TASK

Boldface text

before

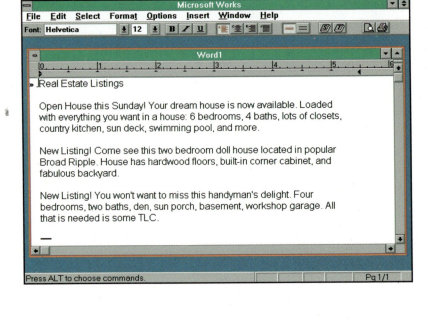

Oops!
To undo the formatting change, select Edit Undo immediately.

1. **Click before the *R* in *Real Estate Listings*.**

   This step places the insertion point at the start of the text that you want to make bold.

   Remember to type any text that appears in the Before screen before you begin this exercise.

2. **Select the entire line.**

   You can use either the mouse or the keyboard to select text. To use the mouse, hold down the mouse button, drag across the text that you want to select, and then release the mouse button. To use the keyboard, hold down the Shift key and use the arrow keys to select the text. See *TASK: Select text* for more information.

   In this exercise, you make one line of text bold. You can, however, make any amount of text bold; just select the text you want.

3. **Click on Format.**

   This step opens the Format menu. You see a list of Format commands.

4. **Click on Font & Style.**

   This step selects the Font & Style command and displays the Font & Style dialog box. This dialog box includes areas for specifying the font, size, style, and position of the text.

5. **In the Style area, click on Bold.**

   This step selects Bold formatting.

Easy **Works for Windo**

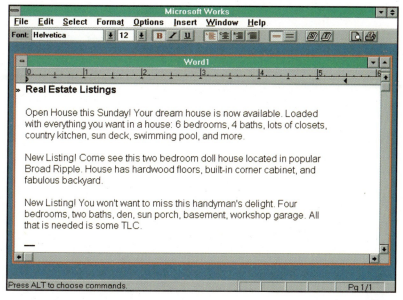

after

Try some shortcuts
Press the Ctrl+B key combination to select the Bold command. Or click on the B icon in the Toolbar to turn on Bold.

6. Click on **OK**.
   This step confirms the choice and closes the dialog box. The selected text is now bold; the text remains selected.

7. Click outside the selected text.
   This step deselects the text.

REVIEW

1. Select the text that you want to make bold.
2. Click on **Format** in the menu bar.
3. Click on the **Font & Style** command.
4. In the Style area, click on the **Bold** option.
5. Click on the **OK** button.
6. Click outside the text.

To boldface text

Turn on bold before you type
To turn on bold before you type, select the Bold option. Type the text that you want to make bold, and then select Bold again to turn off bold.

Word Processing

TASK

Italicize text

Oops!
To undo the formatting change, select Edit Undo immediately.

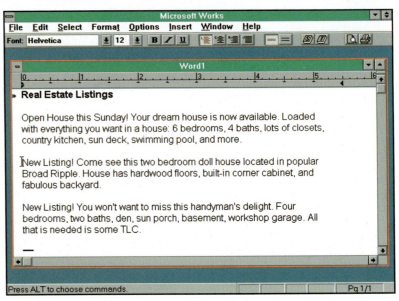

before

1. **Click before the *O* in *Open House*.**

   This step positions the insertion point at the start of the text you want to italicize.

   Remember to type any text that appears in the Before screen before you begin this exercise.

2. **Select the text *Open House this Sunday!***

   You can use either the mouse or the keyboard to select text. To use the mouse, hold down the mouse button, drag across the text that you want to select, and then release the mouse button. To use the keyboard, hold down the Shift key and use the arrow keys to select the text. See *TASK: Select text* for more information.

   In this exercise, you italicize several words. You can italicize any amount of text; just select the text you want.

3. **Click on Format.**

   This step opens the Format menu. You see a list of Format commands.

4. **Click on Font & Style.**

   This step selects the Font & Style command and displays the Font & Style dialog box. This dialog box includes areas for specifying the font, size, style, and position of the text.

Easy Works for Windo

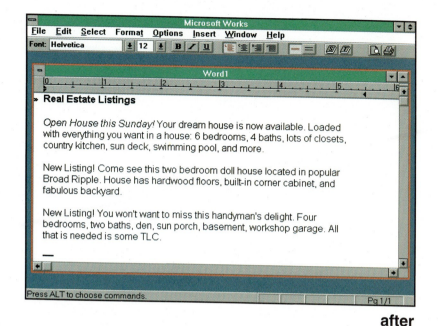

after

Try some shortcuts
Press the Ctrl+I key combination to select the Italic command. Or click on the I icon in the Toolbar to turn on Italic.

5. In the Style area, click on **Italic**.
   This step selects Italic formatting.

6. Click on **OK**.
   This step confirms your choice and closes the dialog box. The selected text is now italicized; the text remains selected.

7. Click outside the text.
   This step deselects the text.

REVIEW

To italicize text

1. Select the text that you want to italicize.
2. Click on **Format** in the menu bar.
3. Click on the **Font & Style** command.
4. In the Style area, click on the **Italic** option.
5. Click on the **OK** button.
6. Click outside the text.

Turn on italic before you type
To turn on italicizing before you type, select the Italic option. Type the text that you want to italicize, and then select Italic again to turn off italicizing.

Word Processing

85

TASK

Underline text

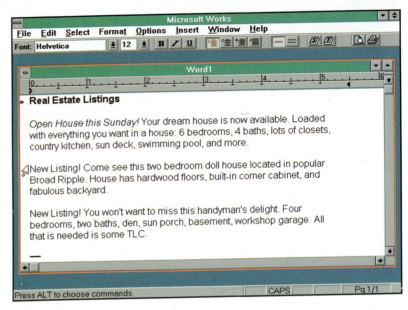

before

Oops!
To undo the formatting change, select Edit Undo immediately.

1. **Click before the** *N* **in** *New Listing* **in the second paragraph.**

   This step places the insertion point at the start of the text that you want to underline.

   Remember to type any text that appears in the Before screen before you begin this exercise.

2. **Select the text** *New Listing!*

   You can use either the mouse or the keyboard to select text. To use the mouse, hold down the mouse button, drag across the text that you want to select, and then release the mouse button. To use the keyboard, hold down the Shift key and use the arrow keys to select the text. See *TASK: Select text* for more information.

   In this exercise, you underline several words. You can, however, underline any amount of text; just select the text you want.

3. **Click on Format.**

   This step opens the Format menu. You see a list of Format commands.

4. **Click on Font & Style.**

   This step selects the Font & Style command and displays the Font & Style dialog box. This dialog box includes areas for specifying the font, size, style, and position of the text.

Easy Works for Windo

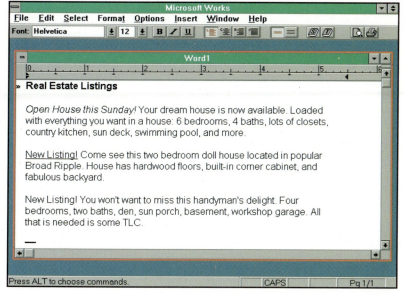

after

Try some shortcuts
Press the Ctrl+U key combination to select the Underline command. Or click on the U icon in the Toolbar to turn on underlining.

Turn on underlining before you type
To turn on underlining before you type, select the Underline option. Type the text that you want to underline, and then select Underline again to turn off underlining.

5. In the Style area, click on **Underline**.
   This step selects Underline formatting.

6. Click on **OK**.
   This step confirms the choice and closes the dialog box. The selected text is now underlined; the text remains selected.

7. Click outside the text.
   This step deselects the text.

REVIEW

To Underline Text

1. Select the text that you want to underline.
2. Click on **Format** in the menu bar.
3. Click on the **Font & Style** command.
4. In the Style area, click on the **Underline** option.
5. Click on the **OK** button.
6. Click outside the text.

TASK

Change the font

before

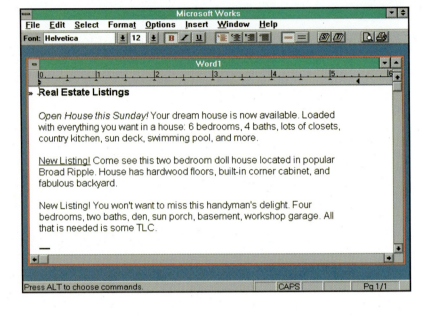

Oops!
To undo the formatting change, select Edit Undo immediately.

1. **Click before the *R* in *Real Estate Listings*.**

   This step places the insertion point at the start of the text that you want to change.

   Remember to type any text that appears in the Before screen before you begin this exercise.

2. **Select the entire line.**

   You can use either the mouse or the keyboard to select text. To use the mouse, hold down the mouse button, drag across the text that you want to select, and then release the mouse button. To use the keyboard, hold down the Shift key and use the arrow keys to select the text. See *TASK: Select text* for more information.

   In this exercise, you change the font of a line of text. You can, however, change any amount of text; just select the text you want.

3. **Click on Format.**

   This step opens the Format menu. You see a list of Format commands.

4. **Click on Font & Style.**

   This step selects the Font & Style command and displays the Font & Style dialog box. This dialog box includes areas for specifying the font, size, style, and position of the text.

88

Easy Works for Windo

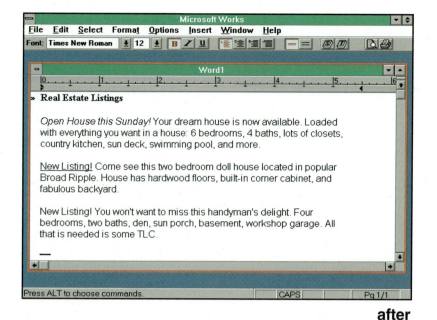

after

Use the Toolbar
You also can use the Toolbar to change the font. Click on the arrow next to the current font name; then click on the font you want.

5. Click on **Times New Roman** in the Font list.
   If you don't have this font, select one that you do have. You may have to scroll through the list to find this font.

6. Click on **OK**.
   This step confirms the new font and returns you to the document. The selected text is displayed in the new font; the text remains selected.

7. Click outside the text.
   This step deselects the text.

REVIEW

To change the font

1. Select the text that you want to change.
2. Click on **Format** in the menu bar.
3. Click on the **Font & Style** command.
4. In the Font list, click on the font you want to use.
5. Click on the **OK** button.
6. Click outside the text.

TASK

Change the font size

before

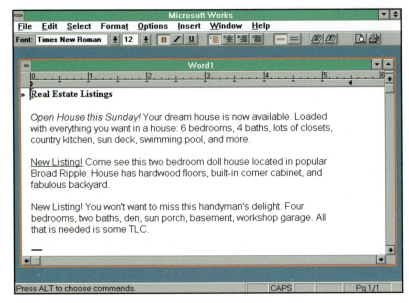

Oops!
To undo the formatting change, select Edit Undo.

1. Click before the *R* in *Real Estate Listings*.

   This step places the insertion point at the start of the text that you want to change.

   Remember to type any text that appears in the Before screen before you begin this exercise.

2. Select the text *Real Estate Listings*.

   You can use either the mouse or the keyboard to select text. To use the mouse, hold down the mouse button, drag across the text that you want to select, and then release the mouse button. To use the keyboard, hold down the Shift key and use the arrow keys to select the text. See *TASK: Select text* for more information.

   In this exercise, you format one line of text. You can, however, change the font size of any amount of text; just select the text you want.

3. Click on **Format**.

   This step opens the Format menu. You see a list of Format commands.

4. Click on **Font & Style**.

   This step selects the Font & Style command and displays the Font & Style dialog box. This dialog box includes areas for specifying the font, size, style, and position of the text.

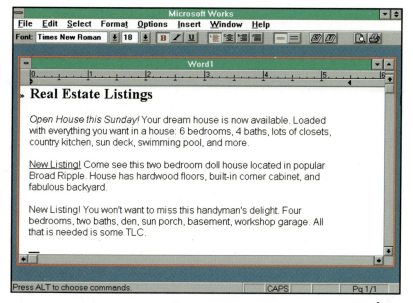

after

Use the Toolbar
You also can use the Toolbar to change the font size. Click on the down arrow next to the current font size; then click on the font size you want.

5. In the Size list, click on **18**.
   This step selects 18-point type. If you don't have this font size, select one that you do have.

6. Click on **OK**.
   This step confirms the new font size and returns you to the document. The selected text appears in the new font size; the text is still selected.

7. Click outside the text.
   This step deselects the text.

REVIEW

To change the font size

1. Select the text you want to change.
2. Click on **Format** in the menu bar.
3. Click on the **Font & Style** command.
4. In the Size list, click on the font size you want to use.
5. Click on the **OK** button.
6. Click outside the text.

TASK

Center text

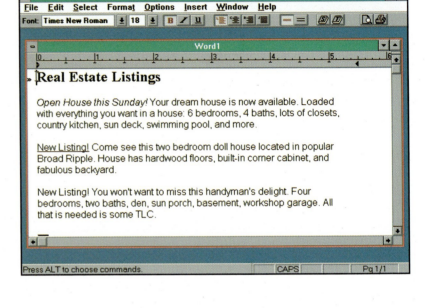

before

Oops!
To undo the formatting change, select Edit Undo immediately.

1. **Click before the *R* in *Real Estate Listings*.**

   This step positions the insertion point at the beginning of the line you want to center.

   Remember to type any text that appears in the Before screen before you begin this exercise.

2. **Click on Format.**

   This step opens the Format menu. You see a list of Format commands.

3. **Click on Indents & Spacing.**

   This step selects the Indents & Spacing command and displays the Indents & Spacing dialog box. This dialog box controls the indents, alignment, spacing, and pagination options for paragraphs.

4. **In the Alignment area, click on Center.**

   This step selects the Center option.

5. **Click on OK.**

   The line is centered on-screen.

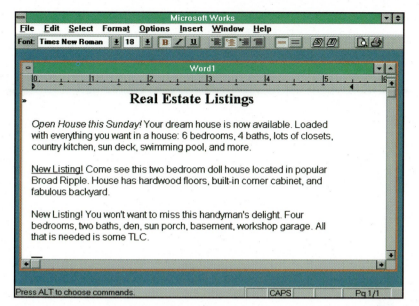

after

Try some shortcuts
Press the Ctrl+E key combination to center a line of text. Or click on the Center icon (the icon displays several centered lines) in the Toolbar.

REVIEW

To center text

1. Position the insertion point at the beginning of the paragraph that you want to center.

2. Click on **Format** in the menu bar.

3. Click on the **Indents & Spacing** command.

4. In the Alignment area, click on **Center**.

5. Click on the **OK** button.

TASK

Indent text

before

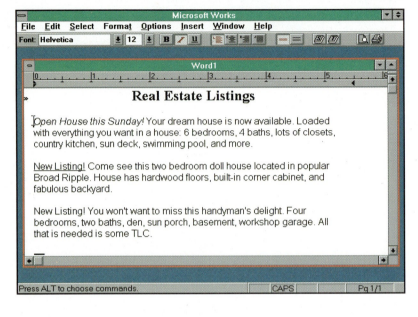

Oops!
To undo the formatting change, select Edit Undo immediately.

1. Click before the *O* in *Open*.

   This step places the insertion point at the start of the paragraph that you want to indent.

   Remember to type any text that appears in the Before screen before you begin this exercise.

   This task indents one paragraph. You can also indent several paragraphs at once. To do so, just select all the paragraphs that you want to indent.

2. Click on **Format**.

   This step opens the Format menu. You see a list of Format commands.

3. Click on **Indents & Spacing**.

   This step selects the Indents & Spacing command and displays the Indents & Spacing dialog box. This dialog box controls the indents, alignment, spacing, and pagination options for paragraphs. The insertion point is positioned in the Left indent text box.

4. Type **.5**.

   This step specifies a half-inch indent.

5. Click on **OK**.

   The text is indented one-half inch from the left margin.

Easy Works for Window

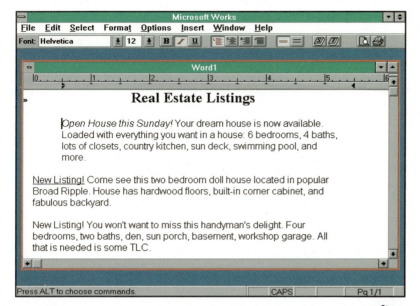

after

1. Position the insertion point at the beginning of the paragraph that you want to indent.

2. Click on **Format** in the menu bar.

3. Click on the **Indents & Spacing** command.

4. In the Left indent text box, type the amount that you want to indent the text.

5. Click on the **OK** button.

Try some shortcuts
Press the Ctrl+N key combination to indent the current paragraph. The text will be indented one-quarter inch. Press the Ctrl+M key combination to undo the indent.

REVIEW

To indent text

Indent before you type
To indent text before you type, use these steps to set the indentation. Then type the text that you want indented.

Word Processing

95

TASK

Check spelling
(Part 1 of 2)

before

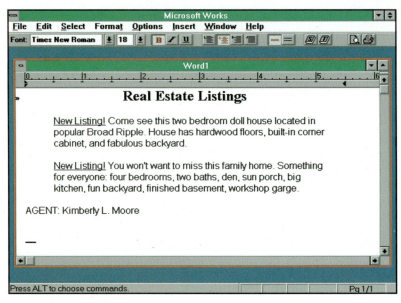

Oops!
To stop a spelling check, when Works stops on a word, click on the Cancel button.

Checking spelling is a two-part process. These two pages cover the first part; turn the page for the second part.

1. Press **Ctrl+Home**.

   Works for Windows starts checking from the location of the insertion point forward. Pressing the Ctrl+Home key combination moves the insertion point to the top of the document so that you can check the spelling in the entire document.

   Remember to type any text that appears in the Before screen before you begin this exercise.

2. Click on **Options**.

   This step opens the Options menu. You see a list of Options commands.

3. Click on **Check Spelling**.

   This step selects the Check Spelling command; Works begins checking your document. (If you have text selected, Works checks only the highlighted text.)

   The Speller compares the words in your document to the words in its dictionary and stops on words it cannot find. (Remember that if Works stops on a word, the word is not necessarily misspelled; it just isn't located in the Works dictionary.)

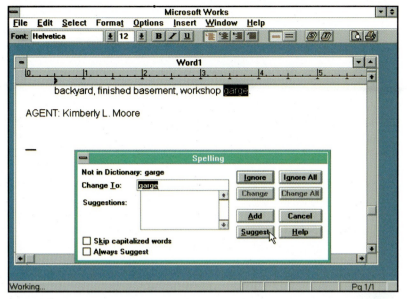

after

What's next?
Checking spelling is a two-part process. Turn the page for the second half of the process.

For this example, Works begins the spell check, stops on the word *garge*, and displays the Spelling dialog area. The word that is not found is displayed in the Not in Dictionary area. Below this area, you see the Change To text box, which lists a suggested spelling. Beneath the text box, you see additional suggestions. The Spelling dialog box includes buttons that enable you to ignore, ignore all, change, change all, suggest spellings, and add the word to the dictionary.

REVIEW

To check spelling
(Part 1 of 2)

1. Press **Ctrl+Home** to start checking spelling at the beginning of the document.
2. Click on **Options** in the menu bar.
3. Click on the **Check Spelling** command.

TASK

Check spelling
(Part 2 of 2)

before

Oops!
To stop a spell check, when Works stops on a word, click on the Cancel button.

Checking spelling is a two-part process. The preceding two pages cover the first part, and these two pages cover the second part.

1. Click on the **Suggest** button.

   This step tells Works to display suggestions in the Suggestion list. The correct spelling, `garage`, appears in the Change To text box.

2. Click on **Change All**.

   This step changes any other occurrences of the word *garge* in the document to *garage*. (If the correct spelling is not selected, click on it in the suggestion list; then click on Change or Change All.)

   The Speller stops on the word *Kimberly*.

3. Click on **Ignore All**.

   This option tells Works to ignore all occurrences of this word; Works will not flag this word again. Works continues to check spelling and stops on the word *Moore*.

4. Click on **Ignore All**.

   This step tells Works to ignore all occurrences of this word.

   A message box appears to alert you that the spelling check is complete.

5. Click on **OK**.

   This step clears the message.

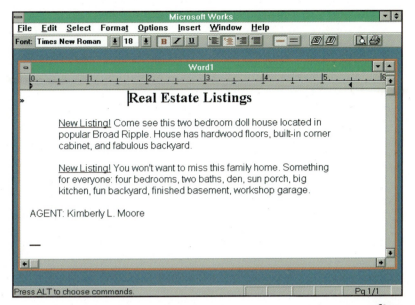
after

Try other options
Works offers many spelling check features. For instance, it can find double words (such as *the the*). Also, you can add words to the dictionary. For complete information, see *Using Works for Windows*.

REVIEW

To check spelling
(Part 2 of 2)

1. When Works stops on a word, select an option:

    Ignore skips this occurrence of the word, but stops on the next one.

    Ignore All skips all occurrences of this word.

    Change replaces this occurrence of the word with the word listed in the Change To text box.

    Change All replaces all occurrences of the word with the word listed in the Change To text box.

    Add adds the word to the dictionary.

    Suggest lists suggestions. If the corrected word is listed in the Suggestion list, click on it and then click on **Change** or **Change All**.

2. Click on the **OK** button when you receive the message that the spelling check is complete.

Use the Always Suggest check box
If you want Works to always suggest alternative spellings, click on the Always Suggest check box in the Spelling dialog box.

Word Processing

TASK

Search for text

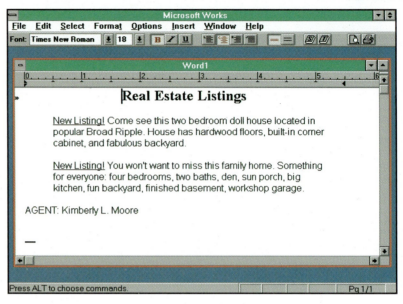

before

Oops!
If the text isn't found, you see the message `No match found`. You might have typed the text incorrectly. Click on OK, check your typing, and try the search again.

1. **Press Ctrl+Home.**

   Works for Windows starts searching from the location of the insertion point forward. Pressing the Ctrl+Home key combination moves the insertion point to the top of the document.

   Remember to type any text that appears in the Before screen before you begin this exercise.

2. **Click on Select.**

   This step opens the Select menu. You see a list of Select commands.

3. **Click on Find.**

   This step selects the Find command. You see the Find dialog box. This box includes the Find What text box and other options that control how the document is searched. (See *Using Works for Windows* for complete information on all the options.) The insertion point is positioned in the Find What text box.

4. **Type family.**

   This text, called the *search string*, is what you want to find.

   By default, Works will find all occurrences of this text—regardless of the case (uppercase or lowercase). You can specify to find only whole words or a search string that matches the exact upper- and lowercase combination that you typed. See *Using Works for Windows* for complete information.

100

Easy **Works for Windows**

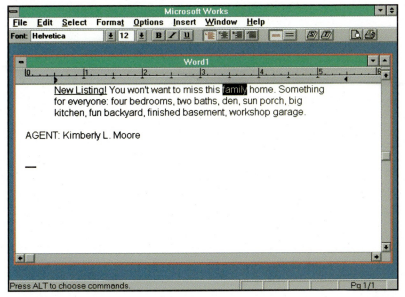

after

Search again
To search for the next occurrence of the search string, press the F7 key.

5. Click on **OK**.

    This step starts the search. The insertion point moves to the first occurrence of the search string. Notice in the After figure that the document has scrolled so that the found word is at the top of the window.

REVIEW

To search for text

1. Press **Ctrl+Home** to move to the beginning of the document.
2. Click on **Select** in the menu bar.
3. Click on the **Find** command.
4. Type the text you want to find.
5. Click on the **OK** button to start the search.

Word Processing

TASK

Replace text
(Part 1 of 2)

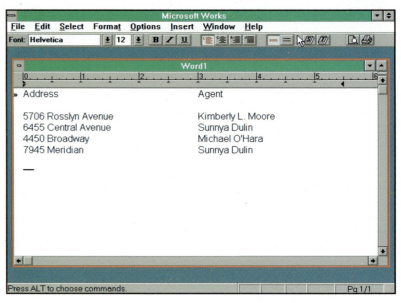

before

Oops!
If the text isn't found, you see the message `No match found`. You might have typed the text incorrectly. Click on OK, check your typing, and try again.

Replacing text is a two-part process. These two pages cover the first part; turn the page for the second part.

1. Press **Ctrl+Home**.

   Works for Windows starts searching from the location of the insertion point forward. This step moves the insertion point to the top of the document.

   Remember to type any text that appears in the Before screen before you begin this exercise.

2. Click on **Select**.

   This step opens the Select menu. You see a list of Select commands.

3. Click on **Replace**.

   This step selects the Replace command. You see the Replace dialog box. This box includes the Find What text box, Replace With text box, and other options that control how the replace is performed. (See *Using Works for Windows* for complete information concerning all the options.) The insertion point is positioned in the Find What text box.

4. Type **Sunnya Dulin**.

   This text, called the *search string*, is what you want to find.

102

Easy Works for Windows

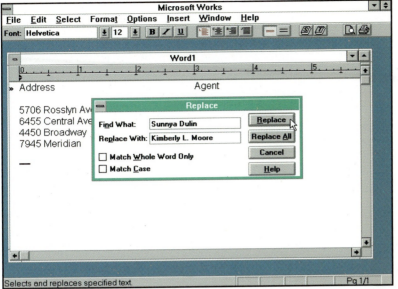

after

What's next?
Replacing text is a two-part process. Turn the page for the second part of the process.

5. Click in the Replace With text box.
   This step positions the insertion point in the Replace With text box so that you can type the replace string.

6. Type **Kimberly L. Moore**.
   This step specifies the text you want to use as the replacement.

REVIEW

To replace text
(Part 1 of 2)

1. Press **Ctrl+Home** to move to the beginning of the document.
2. Click on **Select** in the menu bar.
3. Click on the **Replace** command.
4. In the Find What text box, type the text that you want to replace.
5. Click in the Replace With text box.
6. Type the text you want to use as the replacement.

Word Processing

103

TASK

Replace text
(Part 2 of 2)

before

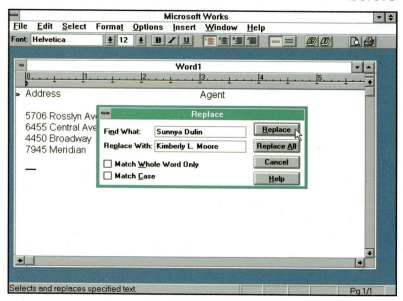

Oops!
If the text isn't found, you see the message `No match found`. You might have typed the text incorrectly. Click on OK, check your typing, and try again.

Replacing text is a two-part process. The preceding two pages cover the first part, and these two pages cover the second part.

1. Click on **Replace**.

   This step selects the Replace button and starts the search. The insertion point moves to the first occurrence of the search string, and the text is selected. A dialog box prompts you with the question, `Replace this occurrence?`

2. Click on **Yes**.

   This step selects the Yes button. The found text is replaced with the new text. Works for Windows moves to the next occurrence and again displays the dialog box.

3. Click on **Yes**.

   This step selects the Yes button and replaces the next occurrence of the text.

   When no more occurrences are found, an alert box appears that states `No more occurrences.`

4. Click on **OK**.

   This step closes the alert box.

5. Press **Ctrl+Home**.

   This step moves the insertion point to the top of the document so that you can see all the changes.

Easy **Works for Windows**

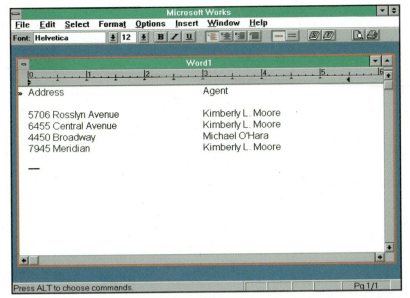

after

1. Click on the **Replace** button to start the search.
2. Click on **Yes** until you make all the replacements.
3. Click on the **OK** button to close the alert box.

Replace All

If you want to make all replacements automatically, click on Replace All for step 7 of the Task section. Before clicking on this option, be sure that you want to replace all occurrences. Every occurrence of the search sting will be replaced by the replacement text.

REVIEW

To replace text
(Part 2 of 2)

TASK

Save a document

before

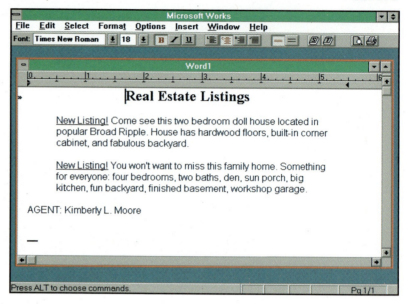

Oops!
If you don't want to save the file, click on Cancel for step 4 of the Task section.

1. Click on **File**.

   This step opens the File menu. You see a list of File commands.

2. Click on **Save**.

   This step selects the Save command. The first time that you save a file, the Save As dialog box appears. This dialog box displays a file list, a directory list, a drop-down drive list, and a drop-down file type list. The insertion point is positioned in the File Name text box so that you can type a file name.

   For information on the other dialog box options, see *Using Works for Windows*.

3. Type **LISTINGS**.

   LISTINGS is the name you want to assign to the file.

   A file name consists of two parts: the file name and the extension. For the file name, you can type up to eight characters. The optional extension, which can be up to three characters, usually indicates the type of file. A period separates the file name and the extension. As a general rule, use only letters and numbers for file names.

   Works automatically assigns a WPS extension to the file name, so the file name you assign becomes LISTINGS.WPS.

4. Click on **OK**.

   This step confirms the file name. The file is saved to disk and remains on-screen. The name of the file appears in the title bar at the top of the screen.

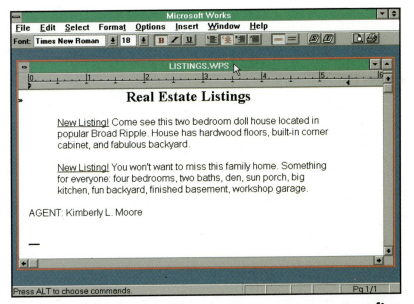
after

Save often
As a general rule, you should save every 5 to 15 minutes. To save the file again, select the File Save command. (Works will not prompt you for a file name after you save and name the file the first time.)

REVIEW

1. Click on **File** in the menu bar.
2. Click on the **Save** command.
3. Type a file name.
4. Click on the **OK** button.

To save a document

Try a shortcut
Press the Ctrl+S key combination to select the File Save command.

Word Processing

TASK

Open a document

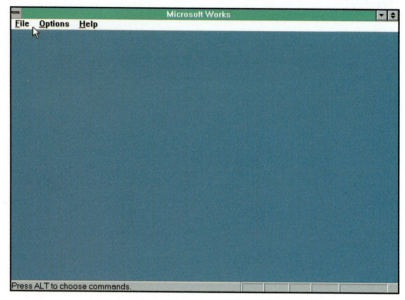

before

Oops!
If you don't want to open the file you selected, click on Cancel for step 4 of the Review section.

1. **Save and close any open documents.**

   For help with this task, see *TASK: Save a document* and *TASK: Close a document window*. You can have more than one document open at a time, but you will save memory and work more quickly with only one document open on-screen.

2. **Click on File.**

   This step opens the File menu. You see a list of File commands.

3. **Click on Open Existing File.**

   This step selects the Open Existing File command. You see the Open dialog box. This box displays a file list, a directory list, and other options. The insertion point is positioned in the File Name text box so that you can type a file name. By default, only files with extensions that start with w (*.w*) are listed. If the file name has a different extension, you will not see the file. See *Using Works for Windows* for information on how to display other file types and how to change drives or directories.

4. **Type LISTINGS.**

   LISTINGS is the name of the file you want to open. You can either type the name or click on the name in the file list.

5. **Click on OK.**

   This step selects the OK button; the document appears on-screen. You see the file name in the title bar.

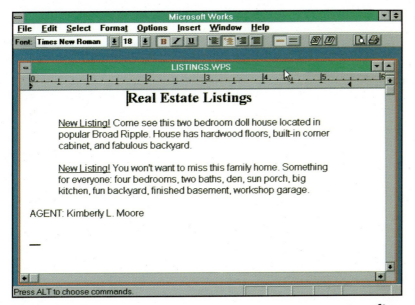

after

Cannot find file?
If you see a message box that tells you `Cannot find file`, click on OK and double-check that you typed the correct file name.

REVIEW

1. Click on **File** in the menu bar.
2. Click on the **Open Existing File** command.
3. Type or click on the name of the file you want to open.
4. Click on the **OK** button.

To open a document

Create a new document
For information on creating a new document, see *TASK: Create a new document.*

Word Processing

109

TASK

Preview a document

before

Oops!
To exit Print Preview, click on the Cancel button.

1. Click on **File**.

   This step opens the File menu. You see a list of File commands.

2. Click on **Print Preview**.

   This step selects the Print Preview command. You see a graphical representation of how your document will look when printed. (The After screen shows this step.)

   From this view, you can print the document or zoom in on a particular part of the document. See *Using Works for Windows* for complete information.

3. Click on **Cancel**.

   This step returns you to the normal document view.

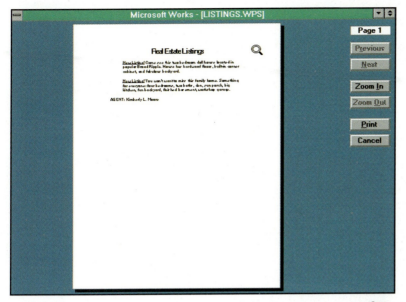

after

REVIEW

1. Click on **File** in the menu bar.
2. Click on the **Print Preview** command.
3. Click on the **Cancel** button.

To preview a document

TASK

Print a document

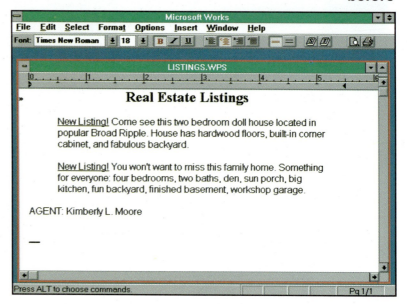

before

Oops!
If you change your mind, click on Cancel for step 3 of the Task section to close the dialog box without printing.

1. Click on **File**.

   This step opens the File menu. You see a list of File commands.

2. Click on **Print**.

   This step selects the Print command. You see the Print dialog box, which enables you to specify the number of copies printed, the print range, and the quality.

3. Click on **OK**.

   This step prints the document.

   The After screen shows a preview of the document, which is an on-screen representation of how the printed document will look.

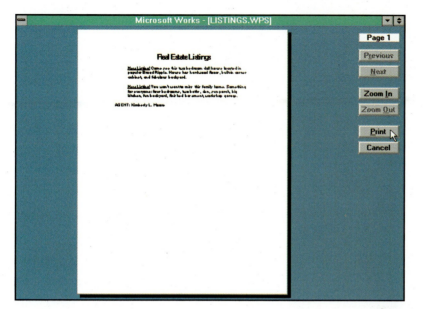

after

Cancel the print job
While the document is printing, a dialog box is displayed on-screen. To cancel the print job, simply click on the Cancel button in the dialog box.

REVIEW

1. Click on **File** in the menu bar.
2. Click on the **Print** command.
3. Change any print options, if necessary.
4. Click on the **OK** button.

To print a document

Try a shortcut
Press the Ctrl+P key combination to select the Print command.

Word Processing

113

Spreadsheet

This section includes the following tasks:

Create a spreadsheet	Copy a formula
Enter text	Set column width
Enter a number	Align text
Enter a date	Format a range
Enter a formula	Make an entry bold
Use a function	Insert a column
Edit a cell entry	Delete a column
Erase a cell entry	Insert a row
Copy a cell entry	Delete a row
Move a cell entry	Save a spreadsheet
Selcect a range	Open a spreadsheet
Copy a range	Preview a spreadsheet
Clear a range	Print a spreadsheet
Move a range	

TASK

Create a spreadsheet

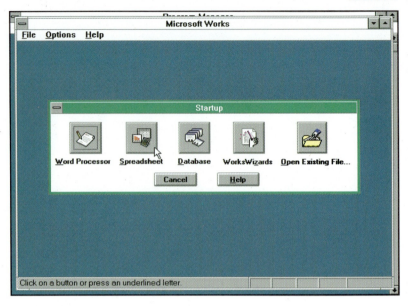

before

Oops!
If you don't want to create a spreadsheet, close the spreadsheet window. See *TASK: Close a document window*.

1. **Start Works for Windows.**

   For help with this step, see *TASK: Start Works for Windows*. You see the Startup dialog box on-screen. The Before screen shows this step.

2. **Click on Spreadsheet.**

   This step selects the spreadsheet tool and displays a blank spreadsheet in a window on-screen. Note that a spreadsheet is a grid of columns and rows. Columns are indicated with letters (A, B, C, and so on), and rows are indicated with numbers (1, 2, 3, and so on). The intersection of a column and row is called a *cell*; you enter information into a cell.

   Along the top of the screen, you see the Toolbar. The *Toolbar* provides access to frequently used commands. To use an icon, click on it. For instance, select a cell and click on the B icon to select the Bold command and make the cell contents bold.

   Below the Toolbar is the *formula bar*. This area displays the current contents of the cell.

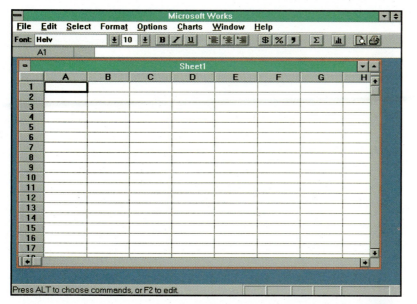

after

Works already started?
If you have already started Works and want to create a document, see *TASK: Create a new document.*

REVIEW

To create a spreadsheet

1. Start Works for Windows.
2. Click on the **Spreadsheet** tool.

TASK

Enter text

before

Oops!
To delete the most recent text entry, see *TASK: Delete a cell entry.*

1. **Click on cell A1.**

   This step makes A1 the active cell. The active cell on a spreadsheet appears as a white cell with a bold border.

   Each cell in a spreadsheet has a unique name. A cell name is formed by combining the column and row locations into one description. For example, A1 describes the intersection of column A and row 1.

   Notice that A1 appears in the Cell reference area to the left of the formula bar.

2. **Type Expenses.**

   This step enters the title of your spreadsheet.

3. **Press Enter.**

   Pressing Enter accepts the entry in the formula bar and enters it into the cell.

   In the formula bar, the entry is preceded by quotation marks, which indicate that the entry is text. Also note that the entry is left-aligned in the cell; this alignment is the default format for text. To change this format, see the tasks on formatting the spreadsheet later in this book.

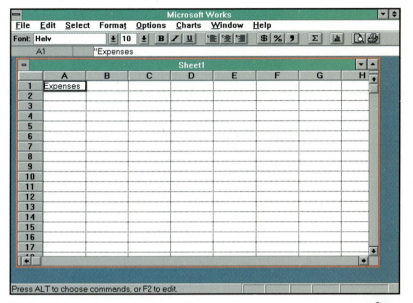

after

1. Click on the cell in which you want to enter text.
2. Type the text.
3. Press **Enter**, **Tab**, or any arrow key.

Use the arrow keys
You also can use the arrow keys to select a cell. And you can press any of the arrow keys or the Tab key to accept the entry and move the active cell.

REVIEW

To enter text

Make a mistake?
If you make a mistake when typing the entry, press the Backspace key once for each character to the left of the cursor that you want to delete. The entry is not placed in the cell until you press Enter or an arrow key.

Spreadsheet

TASK

Enter a number

before

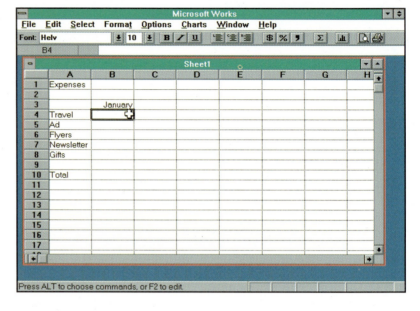

Oops!
To delete a text entry, see
TASK: Erase a cell entry.

1. **Click on cell B4.**

   This step makes B4 the active cell. You see B4 in the Cell reference area to the left of the formula bar.

2. **Type 300.**

   The value—300—appears in the formula bar. If you make a mistake, use the Backspace key to correct the entry. The entry is not placed in the cell until you press Enter or an arrow key.

3. **Press ↓ .**

   This step accepts the entry, enters the value into the cell, and makes B5 the active cell.

   Note that the entry is right-aligned and that no decimal places, commas, or dollar signs are displayed; this is the default format for numbers. To change this format, see other tasks later in this section.

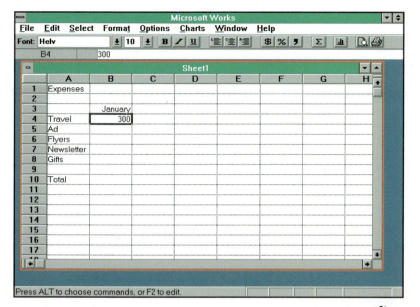

after

Enter a negative number
To enter a negative number, type a minus sign, and then type the number.

REVIEW

To enter a number

1. Click on the cell in which you want to enter the number.

2. Type the number.

3. Press **Enter** or any arrow key.

Spreadsheet

121

TASK

Enter a date

before

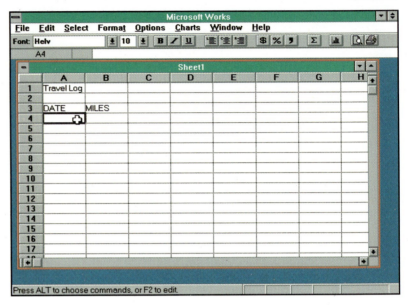

Oops!
If you enter a date in another format (for instance, 8-Aug), Works formats the date as text. You then cannot perform date calculations.

1. **Click on cell A4.**

   This step makes A4 the active cell. You will enter the date into this cell.

   Remember to enter any text that appears in the Before screen before you begin this exercise.

2. **Type 8/14/92.**

   This step enters the date in a format that is acceptable to Works. To enter a date, you must use a format that Works recognizes.

   When you use a date format, Works lets you perform date calculations. (See step 2 of the Review section for available date formats.) For instance, you can subtract two dates.

3. **Press Enter.**

   This step enters the date into the cell.

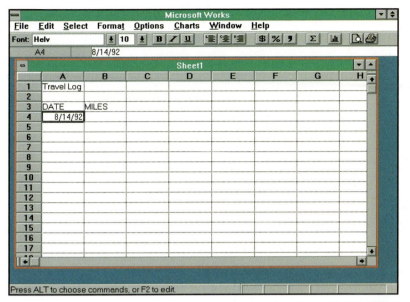

after

See number signs?
If you see number signs (#) in the column, the entry is too large to fit in the column. You must change the column width. See TASK: Set column width.

REVIEW

To enter a date

1. Click on the cell in which you want to enter the date.
2. Type the date in one of these formats:

Format	Example
Month Day, Year	August 14, 1992
Month Year	August 1992
Month Day	August 14
Month	August
MM/DD/YY	8/14/92
MM/YY	8/92
MM/DD	8/14

3. Press **Enter** or any arrow key.

Spreadsheet

123

TASK

Enter a formula

before

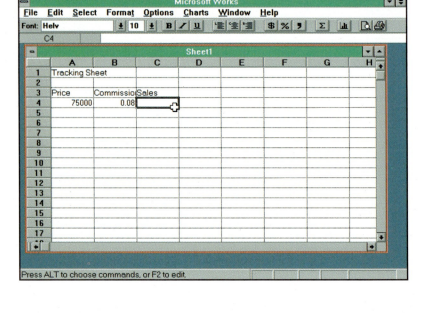

Oops!
To delete a formula, see
TASK: Erase a cell entry.

1. **Click on cell C4.**

   This step makes C4 the active cell. The answer to the formula will appear in this cell.

   Remember to enter any text that appears in the Before screen before you begin this exercise.

2. **Type =.**

   Typing = tells Works that you want to enter a formula. To multiply the contents of two or more cells, you create a multiplication formula by pointing to the cells you want to include in the formula.

3. **Click on cell A4.**

   This step selects cell A4, which is the first cell that you want to include in the multiplication formula. You see =A4 in the formula bar.

4. **Press *.**

   The * sign is the operator. It tells Works which mathematical operation you want to perform—in this case, multiplication.

5. **Click on cell B4.**

   This step selects cell B4, which is the second cell that you want to include. You see =A4*B4 in the formula bar.

124

Easy **Works for Window**

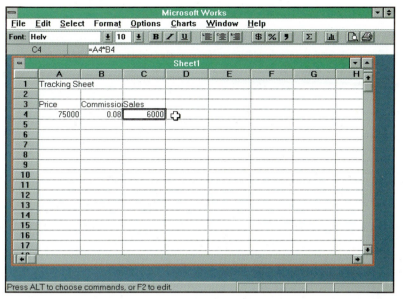

after

What are the benefits of a formula?
You can just type the values that the formula contains, but then if you change the contents of a cell, the result of the formula will be incorrect. Because the formula references the cell that contains the value—rather than the actual value—the formula will change when the value changes. This capability is one of the greatest advantages of an electronic spreadsheet.

6. Press **Enter**.

   Pressing Enter tells Works that you are finished with the formula. You see the results of the formula in cell C4. The formula bar displays the actual formula—not the results.

   You can include any cells in your formula, and you can use different operators (+, −, /). Also, you can combine mathematical operations—for instance, C3+C4−D5. For information on creating complex equations and on the order of precedence (the order in which equations are evaluated), see *Using Works for Windows*.

REVIEW

To enter a formula

1. Click on the cell in which you want to enter the formula.

2. Type **=**.

3. Click on the first cell you want to include.

4. Type the operator (**+**, **−**, *****, **/**).

5. Click on the second cell you want to include.

6. Continue typing the operator and clicking on cells until you finish creating the formula.

7. Press **Enter**.

Use the SUM function
You can also use the SUM function to sum values. See *TASK: Use a function*.

TASK

Use a function

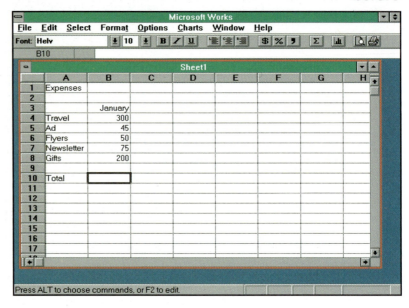

before

Oops!
To undo the formula, delete it. See *TASK: Erase a cell entry*.

1. Click on cell B10.

   This step makes cell B10 the active cell; you will place the function in this cell.

   Remember to enter any text that appears in the Before screen before you begin this exercise.

2. Type **=SUM(**.

   SUM is the name of the function that automatically sums entries. You enter the cells—the range—within the parentheses. (You can type the function in lower- or uppercase letters.)

3. Click on cell B4.

   B4 is the first cell that you want to sum. You see =SUM(B4 in the formula bar and in cell B10.

4. Hold down the mouse button and drag down over cells B5, B6, B7, and B8.

   This step selects the range B4:B8. The formula bar displays =SUM(B4:B8.

   You also can press the Shift key and use the arrow keys to select a range.

Try a shortcut
You also can use the auto-sum tool (Σ) in the Toolbar to quickly create a sum formula. Or press the Ctrl+M key combination. See *Using Works for Windows* for information.

after

5. Type **)**.

   Typing) tells Works that you are finished selecting the range. The range is inserted within the parentheses. In the formula bar, you see =SUM(B4:B8).

6. Press **Enter**.

   Pressing Enter confirms the formula. You see the results of the function in the cell.

What is a function?
A function is a pre-defined formula. You provide the different parts of the formula, and Works calculates the results. Works offers over 57 functions that can help you with tasks ranging from figuring loan payments to calculating investment returns. See *Using Works for Windows* for more information.

REVIEW

1. Click on the cell where you want the sum to appear.

2. Type **=SUM(**.

3. Select the range that you want to sum.

4. Type **)**.

To use a function

Spreadsheet

127

TASK

Edit a cell entry

before

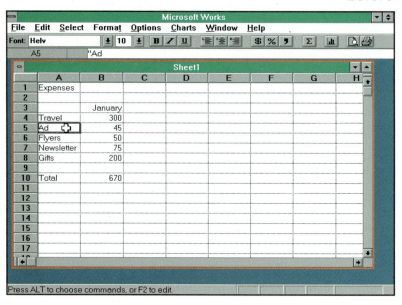

Oops!
Before you press Enter to accept the entry, you can press the Esc key or click the X to cancel the changes.

1. Click on cell **A5**.

   This step makes A5 the active cell. This cell contains the entry that you want to change.

   Remember to enter any text that appears in the Before screen before you begin this exercise.

2. Press **F2**.

   F2 is the Edit key. Pressing this key moves the cursor to the formula bar. The cursor is positioned at the end of the entry. An X and a check mark appear in front of the entry. (Clicking on the X cancels the change; clicking on the check mark confirms the new entry.)

   You also can click directly in the formula bar instead of pressing the F2 key.

   You can use the arrow keys to move the cursor to the characters that you want to change or delete. You also can use the Backspace key to delete characters.

3. Type **vertisements**.

   This step changes this row label from *Ad* to *Advertisements*.

4. Press **Enter**.

   This step accepts the new entry. You cannot see the entire entry because the column is not wide enough. To widen the column so that you can see the entire entry, see *TASK: Set column width*.

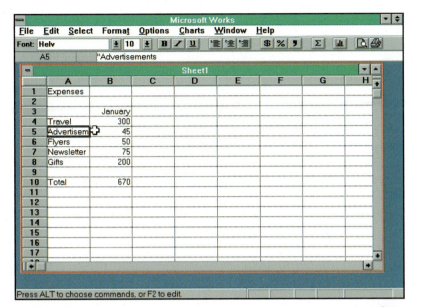
after

Overwrite a cell
When you want to completely change an entry, overwrite the entry. Click on the cell, type the new entry, and then press Enter.

To edit a cell entry

REVIEW

1. Click on the cell whose contents you want to edit.
2. Press **F2** (Edit).
3. Edit the entry in the formula bar.
4. Press **Enter**.

TASK

Erase a cell entry

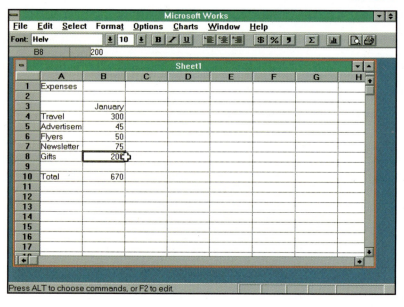

before

Oops!
You cannot undo erasing a cell's entry. If you change your mind after you have erased the entry, retype it.

1. **Click on cell B8.**

   This step makes B8 the active cell; this is the cell whose contents you want to erase. You see the current entry in the formula bar.

   Remember to enter any text that appears in the Before screen before you begin this exercise.

2. **Press Del.**

   Pressing the Del key deletes the entry in the cell.

3. **Press Enter.**

   This step confirms the deletion. If the cell is referenced in any formulas, the formulas will be recalculated.

130

Easy Works for Windows

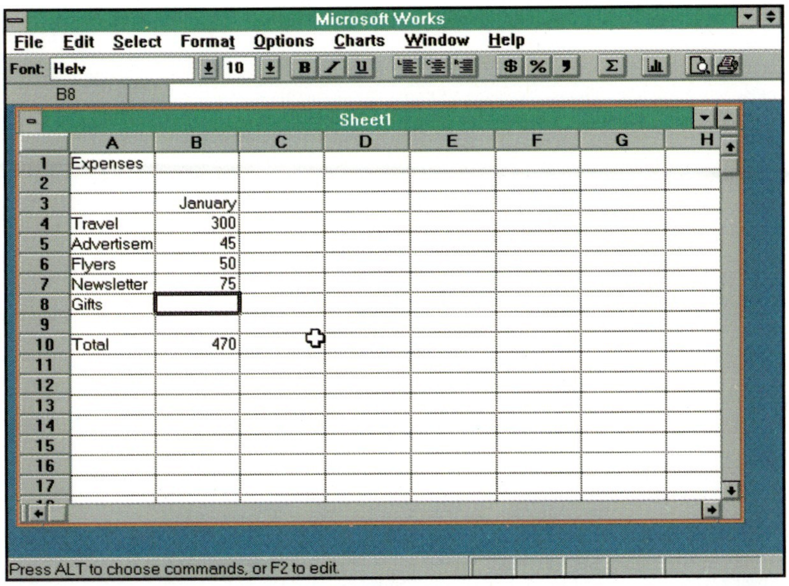

after

1. Click on the cell whose entry you want to erase.
2. Press **Del**.
3. Press **Enter**.

REVIEW

To erase a cell entry

Spreadsheet

TASK

Copy a cell entry

before

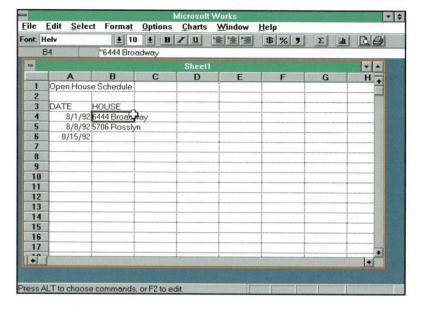

Oops!
To delete the copy, click on the cell that contains the copy and press the Del key.

1. **Click on cell B4.**

   This step makes cell B4 the active cell; this is the cell whose contents you want to copy.

   Remember to enter any text that appears in the Before screen before you begin this exercise.

2. **Click on Edit.**

   This step opens the Edit menu. You see a list of Edit commands.

3. **Click on Copy.**

   This step selects the Copy command.

   Now you need to tell Works where to place the copy.

4. **Click on cell B6.**

   This step makes B6 the active cell. The copy will appear in this cell.

5. **Click on Edit.**

   This step opens the Edit menu.

6. **Click on Paste.**

   This step selects the Paste command. The entry appears in both cells: B4 and B6. Note that Works copies the entry as well as the format (alignment, protection settings, and so on). See other tasks in this section for information on formatting a cell.

   You can also copy the contents in a range (several contiguous cells). See *TASK: Copy a range*.

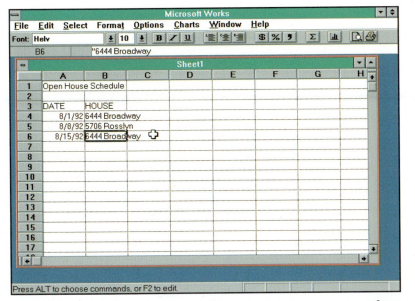

after

Try some shortcuts
Press the Ctrl+C key combination to select the Edit Copy command. Press the Ctrl+V key combination to select the Edit Paste command.

REVIEW

1. Click on the cell whose contents you want to copy.
2. Click on **Edit** in the menu bar.
3. Click on the **Copy** command.
4. Click on the cell in which you want the copy to appear.
5. Click on **Edit** in the menu bar.
6. Click on the **Paste** command.

To copy a cell entry

Spreadsheet

133

TASK

Move a cell entry

before

Oops!
Follow this same procedure to move the entry back to its original location.

1. **Click on cell A8.**

   This step makes A8 the active cell; this is the cell whose contents you want to move.

   Remember to enter any text that appears in the Before screen before you begin this exercise.

2. **Click on Edit.**

   This step opens the Edit menu. You see a list of Edit commands.

3. **Click on Cut.**

   This step selects the Cut command. The entry is cut from the worksheet and moved to the Clipboard. The *Clipboard* is a temporary holding space for text and graphics.

4. **Click on cell A7.**

   This step makes cell A7 the active cell. This is the location where you want the entry to appear.

5. **Click on Edit.**

   This step opens the Edit menu. You see a list of Edit commands.

6. **Click on Paste.**

   This step selects the Paste command. The entry is pasted to the new location.

Easy **Works for Windows**

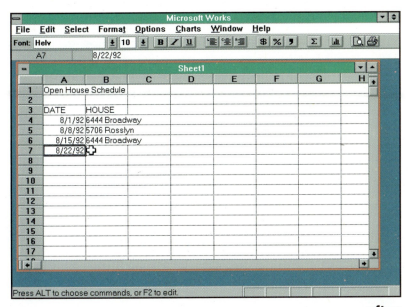

after

1. Click on the cell whose contents you want to move.
2. Click on **Edit** in the menu bar.
3. Click on the **Cut** command.
4. Click on the cell in which you want the entry to appear.
5. Click on **Edit** in the menu bar.
6. Click on the **Paste** command.

Move a range
You also can move the contents in a range (several contiguous cells). See *TASK: Move a range*.

REVIEW

To move a cell entry

Try some shortcuts
Press the Ctrl+X key combination to select the Edit Cut command. Press the Ctrl+V key combination to select the Edit Paste command.

Spreadsheet

135

TASK

Select a range

before

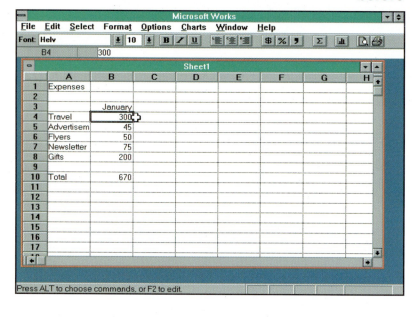

Oops!
To unselect the range, click any cell.

1. **Click on cell B4.**

   This step makes cell B4 the active cell; B4 is the first cell in the range that you want to select. A *range* is any rectangular area of the spreadsheet—a cell, a column, a row, or several columns and rows.

   Remember to enter any text that appears in the Before screen before you begin this exercise.

2. **Hold down the mouse button and drag down the column until you select cells B5, B6, B7, B8, B9, and B10.**

   This steps selects the range B4:B10.

   After you select the range, you can perform other actions, such as format, move, or copy the range. See the other tasks in this section for more information.

Easy **Works for Windows**

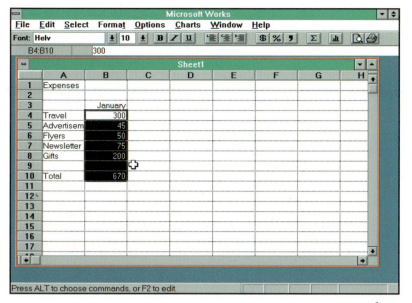

after

1. Click on the first cell that you want to include.

2. Hold down the mouse button and drag across the cells that you want to select.

Try some shortcuts
To select an entire row, click on the row number. To select an entire column, click on the column letter. To select the entire spreadsheet, click on the blank area above row 1 and to the left of column A.

REVIEW

To select a range

Use the keyboard
To use the keyboard to select a range, point to the first cell, hold down the Shift key, and use the arrow keys to highlight the range. You also can use the Select menu to select a range. See *Using Works for Windows*.

Spreadsheet

137

TASK

Copy a range

before

Oops!
To delete the copied range, see *TASK: Clear a range*.

1. **Click on cell B4.**

   This step makes cell B4 the active cell; B4 is the first cell in the range that you want to copy.

   Remember to enter any text that appears in the Before screen before you begin this exercise.

2. **Hold down the mouse button and drag down the column across cells B5, B6, B7, B8, B9, and B10.**

   This step selects the range B4:B10. This is the range that you want to copy.

3. **Click on Edit.**

   This step opens the Edit menu. You see a list of Edit commands.

4. **Click on Copy.**

   This step selects the Copy command. The range is copied to the Clipboard. The *Clipboard* is a temporary holding space for text and graphics.

5. **Click on cell C4.**

   This step selects cell C4; this cell is where you want the first cell of the copied range to begin. The copied range will take the same shape and space as the original; in this case, the copied range will begin at cell C4, and continue over cells C5, C6, C7, C8, C9, and C10. Make sure that the copied range will not overwrite existing data.

Easy **Works for Window**

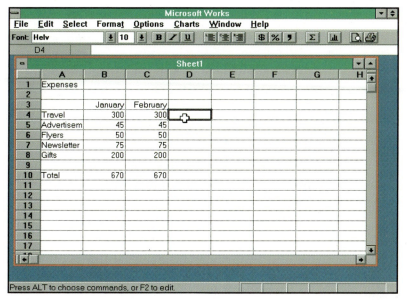

after

Try some shortcuts
Press the Ctrl+C key combination to select the Edit Copy command. Press the Ctrl+V key combination to select the Edit Paste command.

6. Click on **Edit**.
   This step opens the Edit menu. You see a list of Edit commands.

7. Click on **Paste**.
   This step selects the Paste command. The range is copied to the new location. The new range is still selected.

8. Click on any cell.
   This step deselects the range.

REVIEW

To copy a range

1. Select the range that you want to copy.
2. Click on **Edit** in the menu bar.
3. Click on the **Copy** command.
4. Click on the destination—the spot where you want to place the copy of the range.
5. Click on **Edit** in the menu bar.
6. Click on the **Paste** command.

Use the keyboard to select a range
To use the keyboard to select a range, point to the first cell, hold down the Shift key, and use the arrow keys to highlight the range.

Spreadsheet

139

TASK

Clear a range

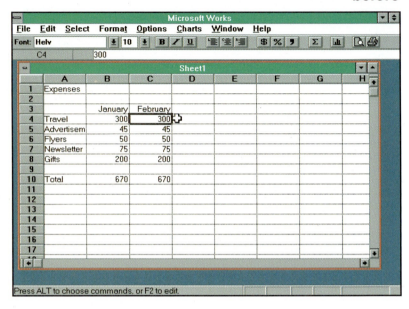

before

Oops!
The spreadsheet tool does not provide an Undo feature. If you delete a range and then change your mind, you must retype the entries.

1. Click on cell C4.

   This step makes cell C4 the active cell; C4 is the first cell in the range that you want to clear (erase).

   Remember to enter any text that appears in the Before screen before you begin this exercise.

2. Hold down the mouse button and drag down the column across cells C5, C6, C7, and C8.

   This step selects the range C4:C8. This is the range that you want to clear.

3. Click on **Edit**.

   This step opens the Edit menu. You see a list of Edit commands.

4. Click on **Clear**.

   This step selects the Clear command. The range is cleared (erased). Cell C10 contains a formula. The column total in cell C10 is adjusted automatically to reflect the new values in the cells. The range is still selected.

5. Click on any cell.

   This step deselects the range.

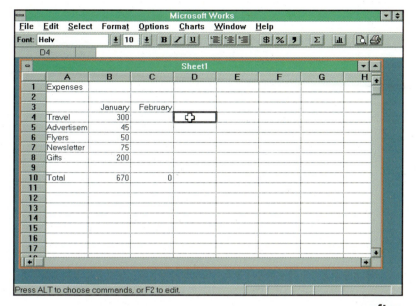

after

Be careful!
When you erase a range that is included in a formula, the formula is recalculated. Be sure that you do not erase any values that are necessary in a formula.

REVIEW

1. Select the range that you want to erase.
2. Click on **Edit** in the menu bar.
3. Click on the **Clear** command.

To clear a range

TASK

Move a range

before

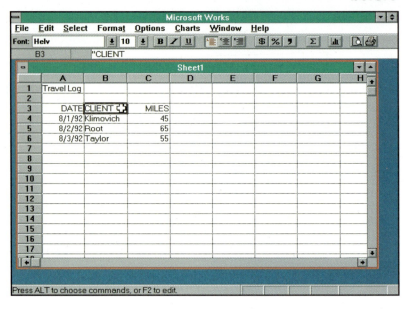

Oops!
To undo the move, follow this same procedure to move the range back to its original location.

1. **Click on cell B3.**

   This step makes cell B3 the active cell; B3 is the first cell in the range that you want to move.

   Remember to enter any text that appears in the Before screen before you begin this exercise.

2. **Hold down the mouse button and drag down the column across cells B4, B5, and B6.**

   This step selects the range B3:B6. This is the range that you want to move.

3. **Click on Edit.**

   This step opens the Edit menu. You see a list of Edit commands.

4. **Click on Cut.**

   This step selects the Cut command. The range is cut from the spreadsheet and placed in the Clipboard. The *Clipboard* is a temporary holding space for text and graphics.

5. **Click on cell D3.**

   This step selects cell D3; this is the first cell where you want to place the range. The range will take the same shape and space as the original; in this case, the range will begin at cell D4, and continue over cells D5, D6, and D7. Make sure that the range will not overwrite existing data.

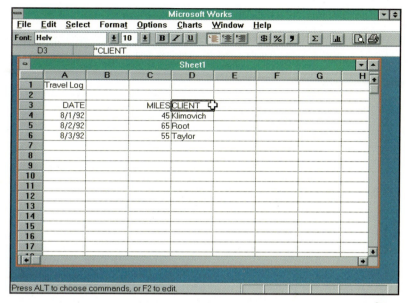

Rearrange the spreadsheet
You can use this process to rearrange the spreadsheet by moving columns and/or rows of information to different places.

after

6. Click on **Edit**.
   This step opens the Edit menu and a list of Edit commands.

7. Click on **Paste**.
   This step selects the Paste command and pastes the selected range to the new location. The range is still selected.

8. Click on any cell.
   This step deselects the range.

REVIEW

To move a range

1. Select the range that you want to move.
2. Click on **Edit** in the menu bar.
3. Click on the **Cut** command.
4. Click on the cell where you want to begin placing the cut range.
5. Click on **Edit** in the menu bar.
6. Click on the **Paste** command.

Use the keyboard to select a range
To use the keyboard to select a range, point to the first cell, hold down the Shift key, and use the arrow keys to highlight the range.

TASK

Copy a formula

before

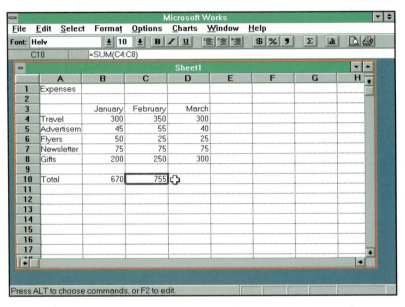

Oops!
To delete the formula, click on the cell that contains the formula and press the Del key.

1. **Click on cell C10.**

   This step makes cell C10 the active cell; C10 contains the formula that you want to copy. (If you have not created this formula, see *TASK: Use a function*.)

   Remember to enter any text that appears in the Before screen before you begin this exercise.

2. **Click on Edit.**

   This step opens the Edit menu. You see a list of Edit commands.

3. **Click on Copy.**

   This step selects the Copy command. The formula is copied to the Clipboard. This *Clipboard* is a temporary holding place for text and graphics.

4. **Click on cell D10.**

   This step selects cell D10; this is the cell where you want the copy to appear.

5. **Click on Edit.**

   This step opens the Edit menu. You see a list of Edit commands.

144   *Easy* Works for Window

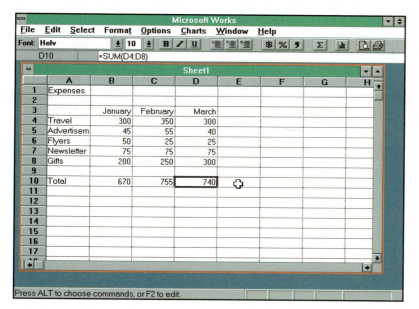

after

Copy a formula to a range
You also can copy a formula to a range of cells. To do so, follow this procedure, but select a range rather than a single cell; then select the Edit Paste command.

6. Click on **Paste**.

    This step selects the Paste command. The results of the formula appear in cell D10. Note that the formula bar contains the formula =SUM(D4:D8). This formula references the current column due to a concept known as *relative addressing*. Works automatically adjusts cell references. For more information on relative addresses, see *Using Works for Windows*.

REVIEW

1. Click on the cell that contains the formula you want to copy.

2. Click on **Edit** in the menu bar.

3. Click on the **Copy** command.

4. Click on the cell where you want the copy to appear.

5. Click on **Edit** in the menu bar.

6. Click on the **Paste** command.

To copy a formula

Try some shortcuts
Press the Ctrl+C key combination to select the Edit Copy command. Press the Ctrl+V key combination to select the Edit Paste command.

145

TASK

Set column width

before

Oops!
Follow this same procedure to change the column width back to its original width (10).

1. **Click on cell A5.**

   This step makes cell A5 the active cell.

   Notice that the entry in cell A5 is currently *truncated*—only part of the entry is displayed. If a cell contains text, the text is longer than the cell, and the cell to the right also includes an entry, then the letters that do not fit in the cell are cut off. When a cell contains a numerical entry that is wider than the cell, the cell displays number signs (#).

   Often formatting (or the selected font) makes the entry longer than the default column width. For instance, 442120 is only six characters long, but if you format the number as currency, with two decimal places, the number appears as $442,120.00. This entry takes 11 spaces. (For information on formatting, see other tasks in this section.)

   You can select any cell in the column that you want to change.

   Remember to enter any text that appears in the Before screen before you begin this exercise.

2. **Click on Format.**

   This step opens the Format menu. You see a list of Format commands.

3. **Click on Column Width.**

   This step selects the Column Width command. You see the Column Width dialog box. The insertion point is positioned in the Width text box. The default column width, 10, is displayed.

after

Use the mouse
To use the mouse to adjust column width, click on the line to the right of the column that you want to widen. Hold down the mouse button. Drag the mouse until the column is the width that you want.

4. Type **15**.
    Typing 15 sets the column width to 15 characters.

5. Click on **OK**.
    This step verifies your selection. The column is widened.

REVIEW

To set column width

1. Click on any cell in the column that you want to change.

2. Click on **Format** in the menu bar.

3. Click on the **Column Width** command.

4. Type the new width.

5. Click on the **OK** button.

147

TASK

Align text

before

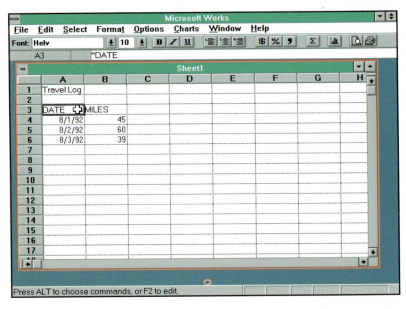

Oops!
To undo the alignment change, follow this procedure and select a new alignment (Left or Center).

1. Click on cell A3.

   This step makes cell A3 the active cell. A3 is the first cell in the range that you want to align.

   Remember to enter any text that appears in the Before screen before you begin this exercise.

2. Hold down the mouse button and drag across cell B3.

   This step selects the range that you want to align: A3:B3.

3. Click on **Format**.

   This step opens the Format menu. You see a list of Format commands.

4. Click on **Style**.

   This step selects the Style command. You see the Style dialog box. This dialog box includes areas for alignment and styles (bold, italic, and so on).

5. Click on **Right**.

   This step selects the Right option.

6. Click on **OK**.

   This step confirms the new choice. Each entry in the range is right-aligned. The range is still selected.

7. Click on any cell.

   This step deselects the range.

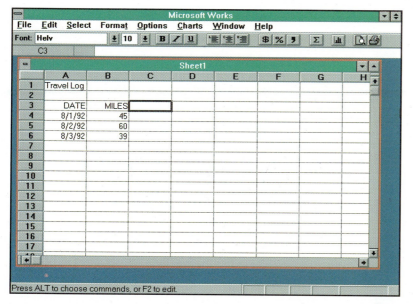
after

Use the Toolbar
Select the range that you want to right-align, and then click on the right-align icon in the Toolbar. This icon has an R and several right-aligned lines.

1. Select the range that you want to align.
2. Click on **Format** in the menu bar.
3. Click on the **Style** command.
4. Click on the **Left**, **Right**, or **Center** option.
5. Click on the **OK** button.

REVIEW

To align text

Center or left-align entries
Follow this same procedure to center or left-align entries. In step 5 of the Task section, click on Center to center text or Left to left-align text.

149

TASK

Format a range

before

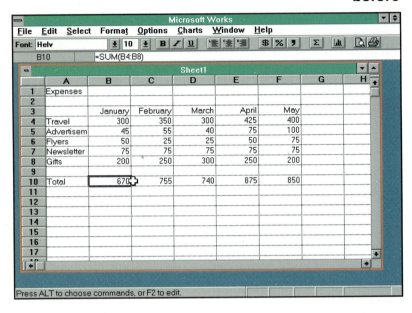

Oops!
To restore the default format, follow this same procedure but select General for step 4 of the Task section.

1. Click on cell B10.

   This step makes cell B10 the active cell. B10 is the first cell in the range that you want to format.

   Remember to enter any text that appears in the Before screen before you begin this exercise.

2. Hold down the mouse button and drag across cells C10, D10, E10, and F10.

   This step selects the range B10:F10. This is the range that you want to format.

3. Click on **Format**.

   This step opens the Format menu. You see a list of Format commands.

4. Click on **Currency**.

   This step selects the Currency command. You see the Currency dialog box. This dialog box prompts you for the number of decimal places. The default is 2.

5. Click on **OK**.

   This step accepts the default number of decimal places and confirms the choice. The range remains selected. (Click any cell to deselect the range.) The formula bar displays the entry as you typed it, but the contents in the cell are formatted to show dollar signs and 2 decimal places.

150

Easy Works for Windo

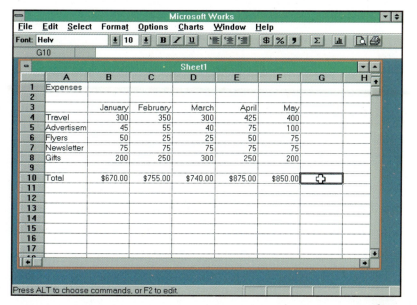

after

Use the Toolbar

You also can select the currency, percentage, and comma formats from the Toolbar. Select the range, and then click on the appropriate icon.

REVIEW

To format a range

1. Select the range that you want to change.

2. Click on **Format** in the menu bar.

3. Click on the format that you want: **General**, **Fixed**, **Currency**, **Comma**, **Percent**, **Exponential**, **Leading Zeros**, or **True/False**.

4. If necessary, type the number of decimal places.

5. Click on the **OK** button.

TASK

Make an entry bold

before

Oops!
To turn off bold formatting, follow this same procedure, but click in the Bold check box to remove the X.

1. **Click on cell A1.**

   This step makes cell A1 the active cell. A1 is the cell that you want to change.

   Remember to enter any text that appears in the Before screen before you begin this exercise.

2. **Click on Format.**

   This step opens the Format menu. You see a list of Format commands.

3. **Click on Style.**

   This step selects the Style command. You see the Style dialog box. This dialog box includes areas for alignment and styles (bold, italic, and so on).

4. **Click on Bold in the Styles area.**

   This step selects Bold formatting. An X appears in the check box.

5. **Click on OK.**

   This step confirms the new choice. The cell contents become bold.

Easy Works for Windows

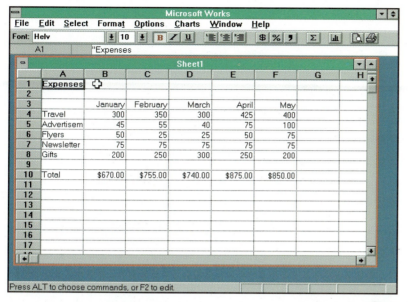

after

Try a shortcut
To apply bold formatting quickly, select the range that you want to make bold and press the Ctrl+B key combination.

REVIEW

To make an entry bold

1. Select the cell or range that you want to change.

2. Click on **Format** in the menu bar.

3. Click on the **Style** command.

4. Click on the **Bold**, **Italic**, or **Underline** check boxes.

5. Click on the **OK** button.

Apply italicizing or underlining
Follow this same procedure to make entries italic or underlined. In step 4 of the Task section, select the style you want. Or press the Ctrl+I (italic) or Ctrl+U (underline) key combination.

TASK

Insert a column

before

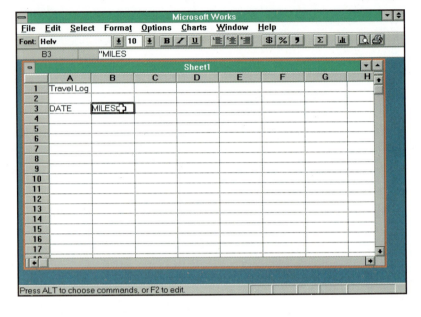

Oops!
To delete a column, see
TASK: Delete a column.

1. **Click on column B.**

   This step selects column B. Be sure to click on the column letter so that you select the entire column. The new column will be inserted to the left of this column.

   Remember to enter any text that appears in the Before screen before you begin this exercise.

2. **Click on Edit.**

   This step opens the Edit menu. You see a list of Edit commands.

3. **Click on Insert Row/Column.**

   This step selects the Insert Row/Column command and inserts a new column. The range remains selected.

4. **Click on any cell.**

   This step deselects the range.

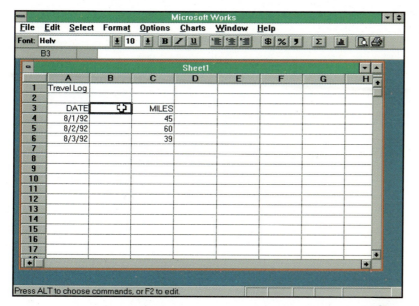

after

See a dialog box?
If you don't select the entire column, the Insert dialog box appears. To insert a column, click on the Column button in the dialog box, and then click on OK.

REVIEW

1. Click on the letter of the column that is right of where you want the new column inserted.
2. Click on **Edit** in the menu bar.
3. Click on the **Insert Row/Column** command.

To insert a column

TASK

Delete a column

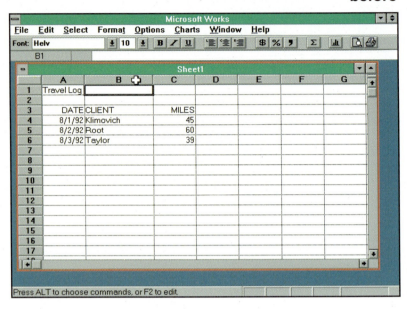

before

Oops!
The spreadsheet tool does not have an Undo command. If you delete a column, the only way to get that column back is to retype the data.

1. Click on column B.

   This step selects column B. Be sure to click on the column letter so that you select the entire column. Column B is the column that you want to delete. All columns to the right of column B will be shifted to the left when this column is deleted.

   Remember to enter any text that appears in the Before screen before you begin this exercise.

2. Click on **Edit**.

   This step opens the Edit menu. You see a list of Edit commands.

3. Click on **Delete Row/Column**.

   This step selects the Delete Row/Column command and deletes the column. The other columns move over to fill in the gap. The next column is selected.

4. Click on any cell.

   This step deselects the column.

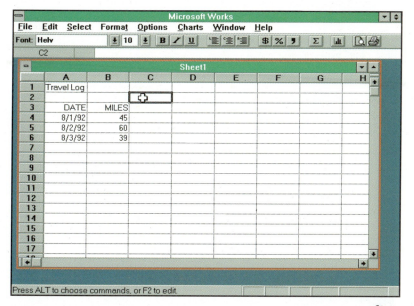

after

Be careful!
When you delete a column, you delete all the data in that column—including any data that is off the screen. Be sure to check the entire column before you delete it.

1. Select the entire column that you want to delete by clicking on the column letter.
2. Click on **Edit** in the menu bar.
3. Click on the **Delete Row/Column** command.

REVIEW

To delete a column

See a dialog box?
If you don't select the entire column, the Delete dialog box appears. To delete a column, click on the Column button in the dialog box, and then click on OK.

157

TASK

Insert a row

before

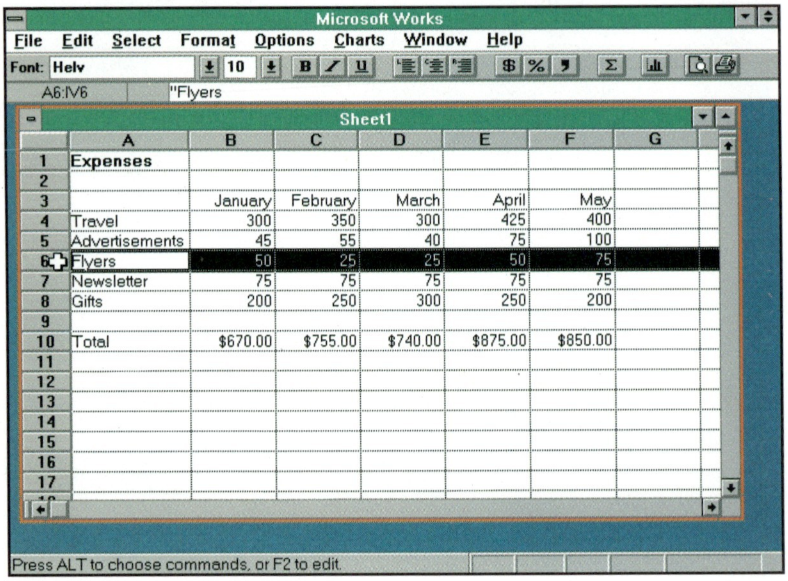

[Screenshot of Microsoft Works spreadsheet showing Expenses data with row 6 "Flyers" selected]

Oops!
To delete the new row, see *TASK: Delete a row*.

1. **Click on row 6.**

   This step selects row 6. Click on the row number, not a cell in the row. The new row will be inserted above the selected row.

   Remember to enter any text that appears in the Before screen before you begin this exercise.

2. **Click on Edit.**

   This step opens the Edit menu. You see a list of Edit commands.

3. **Click on Insert Row/Column.**

   This step selects the Insert Row/Column command and inserts the new row. The range remains selected.

4. **Click on any cell.**

   This step deselects the selected row.

Easy Works for Windows

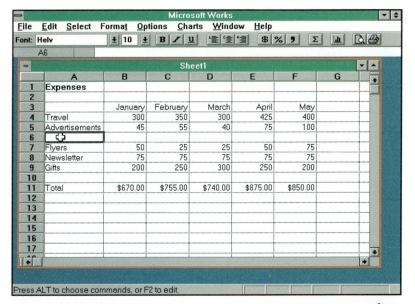

after

See a dialog box?
If you don't select the entire row, the Insert dialog box appears. To insert a row, click on the Row button in the dialog box, and then click on OK.

REVIEW

1. Click on the number of the row that is below where you want the new row inserted.

2. Click on **Edit** in the menu bar.

3. Click on the **Insert Row/Column** command.

To insert a row

TASK

Delete a row

before

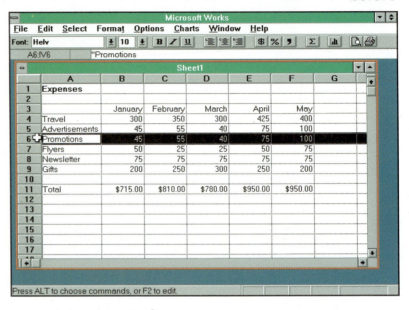

Oops!
The spreadsheet tool does not have an Undo command. If you delete a row, the only way to get that row back is to retype the data.

1. Click on row 6.

   This step selects row 6, which is the row that you want to delete. Be sure to click on the row number so that you will select the entire row.

   Remember to enter any text that appears in the Before screen before you begin this exercise.

2. Click on **Edit**.

   This step opens the Edit menu. You see a list of Edit commands.

3. Click on **Delete Row/Column**.

   This step selects the Delete Row/Column command and deletes the row. The other rows move up to fill in the gap. The range remains selected.

4. Click on any cell.

   This step deselects the selected row.

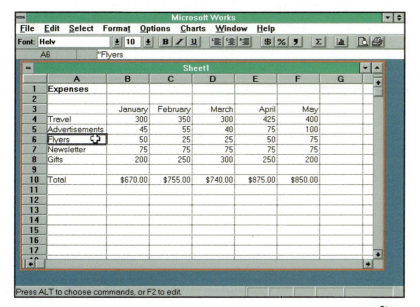

after

1. Click on the number of the row that you want to delete.
2. Click on **Edit** in the menu bar.
3. Click on the **Delete** command.

Be careful!
When you delete the row, you delete all the data in that row—including any data that is off the screen. Be sure that you check the entire row before you delete it.

REVIEW

To delete a row

See a dialog box?
If you don't select the entire row, the Delete dialog box appears. To delete a row, click on the Row button in the dialog box, and then click on OK.

TASK

Save a spreadsheet

before

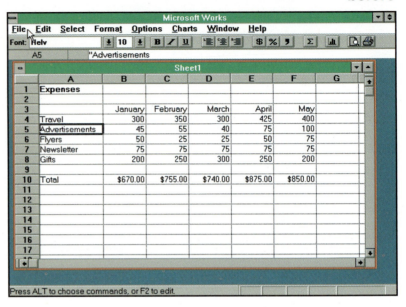

Oops!
If you type a file name that already exists, you see an alert box that warns, Replace existing file? Click Cancel to return to the dialog box, and then type a new name.

1. Click on **File**.

   This step opens the File menu. You see a list of File commands.

2. Click on **Save**.

   This step selects the Save command. When you save the file for the first time, the Save As dialog box appears. This box displays a file list, a directory list, a drop-down Drive list, and a drop-down File Type list. The insertion point is positioned in the File Name text box so that you can type a file name.

   For information on the other dialog box options, see *Using Works for Windows*.

3. Type **EXPENSES**.

   EXPENSES is the name you want to assign the file. Works will automatically assign a WKS extension. A file name consists of two parts: the file name and the extension. For the file name, you can type up to eight characters. The extension, which can be up to three characters and is optional, usually indicates the type of file. A period separates the file name and the extension. As a general rule, use only letters and numbers for file names.

4. Click on **OK**.

   This step verifies the file name and returns you to the spreadsheet. In the title bar, you see the file name, EXPENSES.WKS.

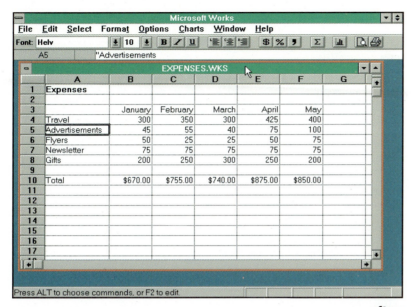
after

1. Click on **File** in the menu bar.
2. Click on the **Save** command.
3. Type the file name.
4. Click on the **OK** button.

Save often
As a general rule, you should save every 5 to 15 minutes. To save the file again, select the File Save command. (Works will not prompt you for a file name.) Until you save the spreadsheet, the data is not committed to disk. You can lose the data if something happens, such as a power loss.

REVIEW

To save a spreadsheet

Try a shortcut
Press the Ctrl+S key combination to select the File Save command.

TASK

Open a spreadsheet

before

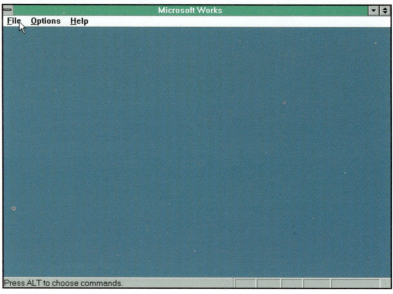

Oops!
If you don't want to open the file, click on Cancel for step 4 of the Review section.

1. **Save and close any open documents.**
   For help with this task, see *TASK: Save a document* and *TASK: Close a document window*. You can have more than one document open at a time, but you will save memory and work more quickly if only the document that you want is open on-screen.

2. **Click on File.**
   This step selects the File menu. You see a list of File commands.

3. **Click on Open Existing File.**
   This step selects the Open Existing File command. You see the Open dialog box. This box displays a File list, a Directory list, and other options. The insertion point is positioned in the File Name text box so that you can type a file name.

   By default, only files with extensions that start with *w* (*.w*) are listed. If the file name has a different extension, you will not see the file. See *Using Works for Windows* for information on how to display other file types and how to change drives or directories.

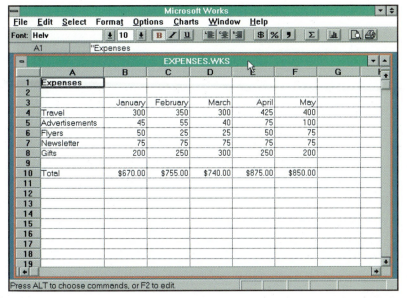

after

Try a shortcut
To open a file quickly, double-click on the file name in the Open dialog box.

4. Type **EXPENSES**.

   EXPENSES is the name of the file that you want to open. You can type the file name if you know it, or you can point to the file name in the Files list by using the mouse or the arrow keys. You do not have to type the extension.

5. Click on **OK**.

   The spreadsheet is opened and appears on-screen. The file name appears in the title bar.

REVIEW

1. Click on **File** in the menu bar.
2. Click on the **Open** command.
3. Type or point to the file name.
4. Click on the **OK** button.

To open a spreadsheet

File not found?
If a message box appears to inform you `Cannot find file`, click on OK and double-check that you typed the file name correctly.

Spreadsheet

165

TASK

Preview a spreadsheet

before

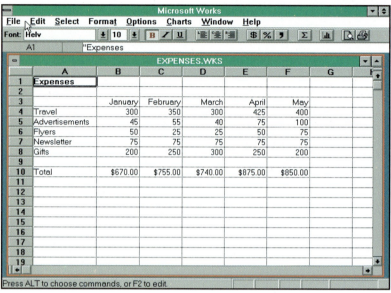

Oops!
To quit the preview, press the Esc key or click on the Cancel button.

1. Click on **File**.

   This step opens the File menu. You see a list of File commands.

2. Click on **Print Preview**.

   This step selects the Print Preview command. You see a preview of your spreadsheet as it will look when printed.

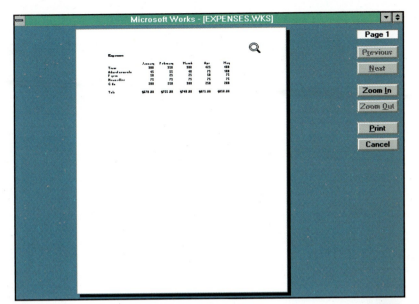

after

1. Click on **File** in the menu bar.
2. Click on the **Print Preview** command.
3. Click on the **Cancel** button to close the preview.

Try some options
You can zoom in and out of the preview or print from the preview. For more information, See *Using Works for Windows*.

REVIEW

To preview a spreadsheet

Try a Toolbar shortcut
Use the Print Preview button on the Toolbar to preview a spreadsheet. (The icon looks like a document with a magnifying glass.)

Spreadsheet

TASK

Print a spreadsheet

before

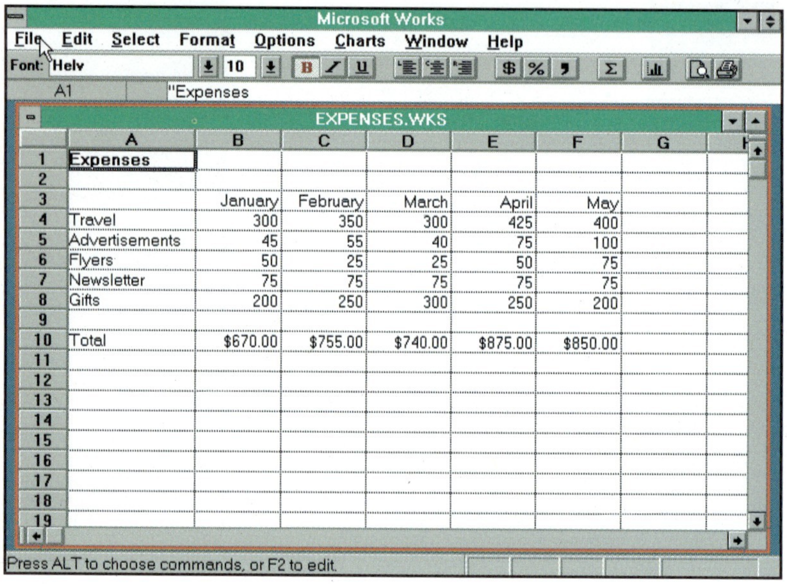

Oops!
If you don't want to print the document, click on Cancel for step 3.

1. Click on **File**.

   This step opens the File menu. You see a list of File commands.

2. Click on **Print**.

   This step selects the Print command. You see the Print dialog box. This dialog box lets you specify the number of copies to print, the page range, and the text quality.

3. Click on **OK**.

   This step starts the print job. The After figure shows a preview of the document, which is an on-screen representation of how the printed document will look.

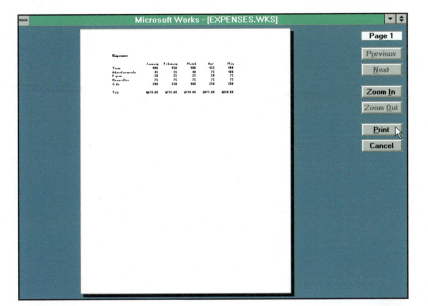

after

Try a shortcut
Press the Ctrl+P key combination to select the Print command. Or click on the Print icon in the Toolbar. (The Print icon has a picture of a printer.)

REVIEW

1. Click on **File** in the menu.
2. Click on the **Print** command.
3. Click on the **OK** button.

To print a spreadsheet

Spreadsheet

169

Database

This section includes the following tasks:

Create a database

Add a label

Enter a field name

Add a field

Edit a field name

Move a field

Change the size of a field

Delete a field

Save a database

Open a database

Enter a record in form view

Add a record in form view

Display a record in form view

Edit a record in form view

Find a record in form view

Delete a record in form view

Change to list view

Change the field width

Add a record in list view

Edit a record in list view

Delete a record in list view

Sort records

Preview a database

Print a database

TASK

Create a database

before

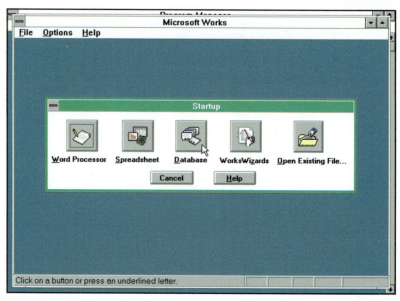

Oops!
If you don't want to create a database after all, close the database window. See *TASK: Close a document window*.

1. **Start Works for Windows.**

   For help with this step see *TASK: Start Works for Windows*. You see the Startup dialog box on-screen. The Before screen shows this step.

2. **Click on Database.**

   This step selects the database tool and displays a blank form in a window on-screen. Note that you can view your database in two views: form view (one record at a time) and list view (several records at a time).

   Along the top of the screen, you see the Toolbar. The Toolbar provides access to frequently used commands. To use an icon, click on it. For instance, select a field and click on the B icon to select the Bold command.

   Below the Toolbar is the formula bar. This area displays the current contents of the field as well as the vertical and horizontal position of the insertion point.

   The area within the window is the work area. You add fields to the database in this area.

   The bottom of the window displays arrows that enable you to navigate among the records. (You do not have any records when you first create a database.)

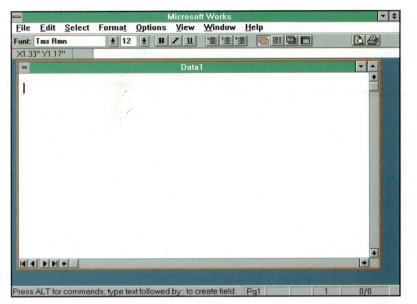
after

Works already started?
If you have already started Works and want to create a document, see *TASK: Create a new document*.

1. Start Works for Windows.
2. Click on the **Database** tool.

REVIEW

To create a database

TASK

Add a label

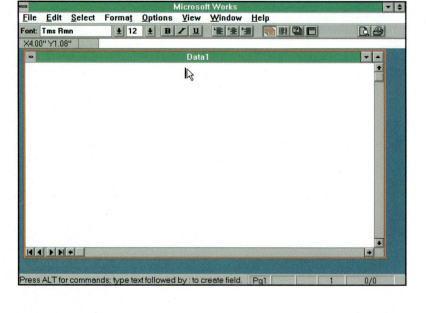

before

Oops!
To delete the label, drag the mouse pointer over the text and then press the Del key.

1. **Click on the center and top of the form.**
   This step places the insertion point where you want to type the label. You can determine the location of the insertion point by looking in the left side of the formula bar. The X position indicates the horizontal position; the Y position indicates the vertical position. The positions are measured from the edges of the page. For this task, place the insertion point at X 4.00" and Y 1.08".

2. **Type Client List.**
   This step enters the label. This label will provide a title for your database. As you type, you see the text on the form and in the formula bar.

3. **Press Enter.**
   Pressing Enter confirms the label.

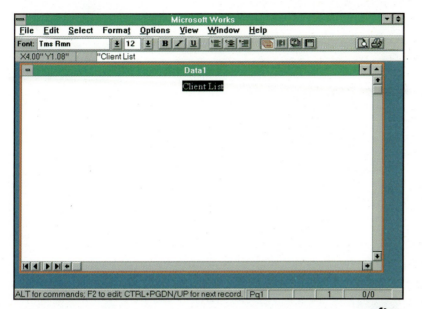

after

Don't use colons
You cannot insert a colon into a label. Works uses colons to identify fields. See *TASK: Enter a field name*.

REVIEW

1. Click the mouse pointer where you want to place the label.
2. Type the label.
3. Press **Enter**.

To add a label

TASK

Enter a field name

before

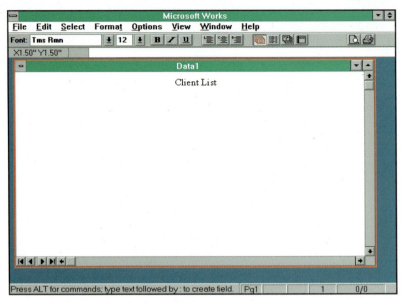

Oops!
To change a field, see
TASK: Change the size of a field and *TASK: Move a field*.

1. Click the insertion point at X 1.50" and Y 1.50".

   This step places the insertion point where you want to enter a field name. You can tell the location of the insertion point by looking in the left side of the formula bar.

2. Type **LAST:**.

   This step enters the field name. Be sure to type the colon. The colon tells Works that this entry is a field name.

3. Press **Enter**.

   This step confirms the field name and displays the Field Size dialog box. You use this dialog box to tell Works how long to make the field. The default width is 20; the default height is 1 line.

4. Click on **OK**.

   This step accepts the default field size. You see an underline on-screen that indicates the field size.

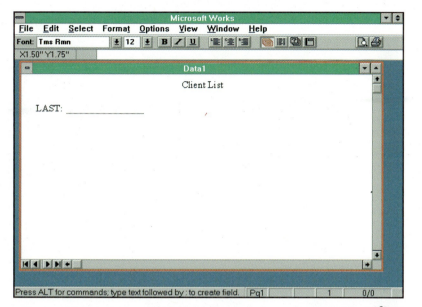

after

What's next?
To add other fields, turn the page for *TASK: Add a field*.

1. Click on the place where you want the field name to appear.
2. Type the field name followed by a colon.
3. Press **Enter**.
4. Enter the width and height for the field.
5. Click on the **OK** button.

REVIEW

To enter a field name

What is a field name?
A *field name* identifies the contents of a field. A *field* is one entry in a record—for instance, the city entry in an address database. A *record* is a set of fields about one particular person, item, or event. For instance, a record in an address database might contain fields for the name, address, city, state, and ZIP code.

TASK

Add a field

before

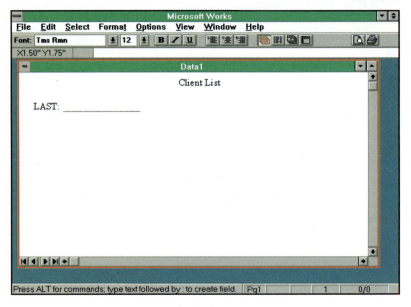

Oops!
To delete a field, see
TASK: Delete a field.

1. Place the insertion point at X 1.50" and Y 1.75".

   This step places the insertion point where you want to enter another field name. You can tell the location of the insertion point by looking in the left side of the formula bar.

   If you have not entered the first field name, see *TASK: Enter a field name*.

2. Type **FIRST NAME:**.

   This step enters the name for this field. Be sure to type the colon. The colon tells Works that this entry is a field name.

3. Press **Enter**.

   This step confirms the field name and displays the Field Size dialog box. You use this dialog box to tell Works how long to make the field. The default width is 20; the default height is 1 line.

4. Click on **OK**.

   This step accepts the default field size. You see an underline on-screen that indicates the field size.

5. Follow steps 1 through 4 to add the following fields:

Field Name	X Position	Y Position	Field Size
ADDRESS:	1.50"	2.00"	20
CITY:	1.50"	2.25"	20

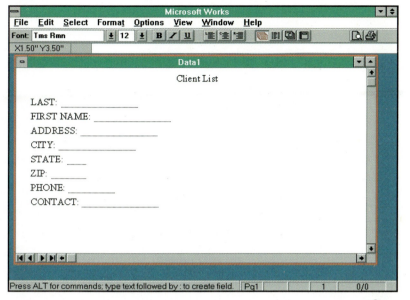

after

STATE:	1.50"	2.50"	5
ZIP:	1.50"	2.75"	9
PHONE:	1.50"	3.00"	12
CONTACT:	1.50"	3.25"	20

This step adds the remaining fields. If you press Enter after entering the field size, you shouldn't have to reposition the insertion point.

Plan your fields
You should sketch out your database on paper before you begin entering fields. Also, you will probably want to create separate fields for some information. Rather than create one address field, for example, you should include separate fields for address, city, state, and ZIP code in case you want to sort the database by one of these fields.

REVIEW

To add a field

1. Click the mouse pointer where you want to add the field.
2. Type the field name; be sure to type a colon at the end of the field name.
3. Press **Enter**.
4. Type the field size.
5. Click on the **OK** button.

Change a field
To change a field, see *TASK: Change the size of a field* or *TASK: Move a field*.

Database

179

TASK

Edit a field name

before

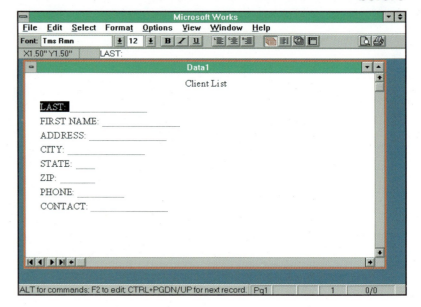

Oops!
If you change your mind, press the Esc key rather than Enter to retain the original name.

1. Click on the LAST field name.
   This step selects the field name that you want to edit. The field appears in reverse video.

2. Type **LAST NAME:**.
   This step enters the new name. Be sure to type the colon.

3. Press **Enter**.
   This step confirms the new name.

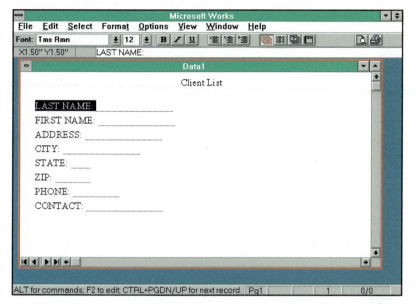
after

What's the limit?
Field names can be up to 15 characters in length.

REVIEW

1. Click on the field name that you want to edit.
2. Type the new name.
3. Press **Enter**.

To edit a field name

TASK

Move a field

before

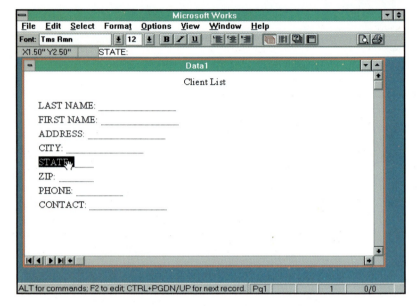

Oops!
Follow this same procedure to restore the field to its original position. No Undo command is available for reversing a move.

1. **Click on the STATE field name.**

   This step selects the field that you want to move. The field appears in reverse video, and when the mouse pointer is positioned on the field, the pointer changes to a hand.

2. **Hold down the mouse button and drag the field to the right of the CITY field.**

   This step moves the field to its new location. Move the field to X position 3.50" and Y position 2.25". You can tell the location of the insertion point by looking in the left side of the formula bar.

3. **Release the mouse button.**

   This step completes the move. After you move one field, you create a gap for other fields. You will probably want to adjust (move) the other fields.

   The remaining examples in this section show the other fields adjusted to accommodate the moved STATE field.

182

Easy Works for Windows

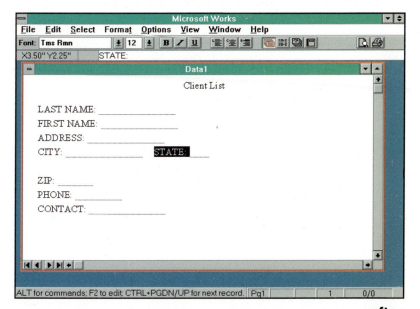
after

1. Click on the field that you want to move.

2. Hold down the mouse button and drag the field to a new location.

3. Release the mouse button.

Use a command
You also can use the Edit Position Field command to specify the exact location where you want to move the field. For information, see *Using Works for Windows*.

REVIEW

To move a field

Rearrange a database
If you want to add fields to the database, you might need to rearrange the current fields to make room. You can follow the steps in this task to rearrange fields.

TASK

Change the size of a field

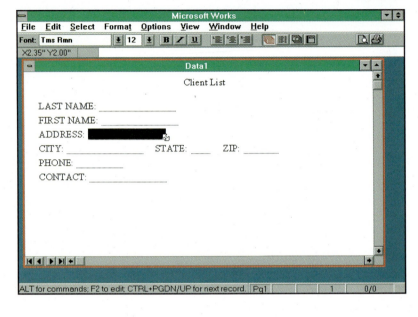

before

Oops!
Follow this same procedure to restore the original field size.

1. Click on the field indicator for the ADDRESS field.
   Do not click on the field name. Instead, click on the underline that indicates the field size. You see a box on-screen. Within that box, there is a small box in the lower right corner. This box is called the *resize box*.

2. Click on the resize box.
   This step selects the resize box, which enables you to change the size of the field. Notice that the mouse pointer changes to a double-headed arrow when you click on the resize box.

3. Hold down the mouse button and drag to the right until the field is the size shown in the After screen.
   This step resizes the field.

4. Release the mouse button.
   This step completes the field size change.

Easy Works for Windo

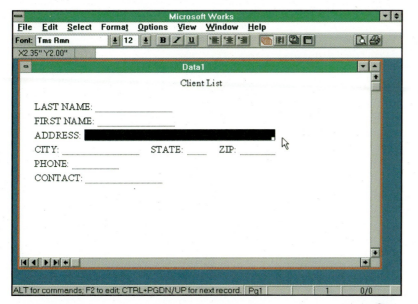

after

1. Click on the field that you want to change.

2. Click on the resize box. Hold down the mouse button and drag to resize the field.

3. Release the mouse button.

Use a menu command
You also can use the Format Field Size command to resize the field. The mouse method allows you to "eyeball" the length. The menu command allows you to type an exact number. See *Using Works for Windows*.

REVIEW

To change the size of a field

Decrease the size of the field
In this task, you increased the field size. You can use this same method to decrease the size of the field. Simply drag to the left rather than to the right.

TASK

Delete a field

before

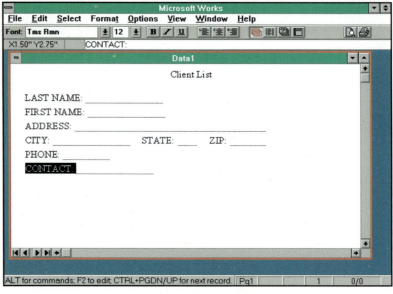

Oops!
To add back the field, see *TASK: Add a field*. You cannot undo the change.

1. **Click on the CONTACT field name.**
   This step selects the field that you want to delete.

2. **Click on Edit.**
   This step opens the Edit menu and displays a list of Edit commands.

3. **Click on Delete Field.**
   This step selects the Delete Field command. You see a dialog box that asks whether it is okay to delete the data in the field. When you delete a field, you also delete any entries that you have made in that field (any records that you have added). In this case, you haven't added any records, so you will not lose any data.

4. **Click on OK.**
   This step confirms the command, and the field is deleted.

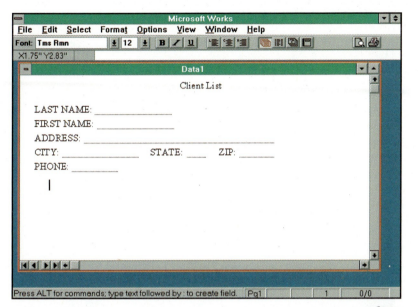
after

Be careful!
Keep in mind that when you delete a field, you also delete any entries that you have made in that field.

REVIEW

To delete a field

1. Click on the field that you want to delete.
2. Click on **Edit** in the menu bar.
3. Click on the **Delete Field** command.
4. Click on the **OK** button.

TASK

Save a database

before

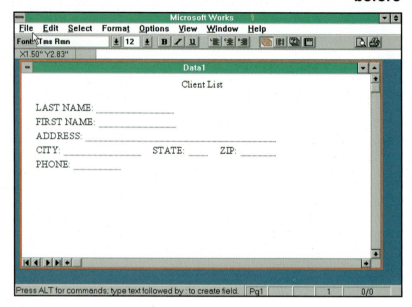

Oops!
If you type a file name that already exists, you see an alert box that prompts, `Replace existing file?` Click on the Cancel button to return to the dialog box; then type a new name for the file.

1. Click on **File**.

   This step opens the File menu. You see a list of File commands. As you create the database, you should save periodically. You should also save as you enter records into the database.

2. Click on **Save**.

   This step selects the Save command. When you save the file for the first time, you see the Save As dialog box. This box displays a file list, a directory list, a drop-down drive list, and a drop-down file type list. The insertion point is positioned in the File Name text box so that you can type a file name.

   For information on the other dialog box options, see *Using Works for Windows*.

3. Type **CLIENTS**.

   CLIENTS is the name you want to assign the file. Works will automatically assign a WDB extension. A file name consists of two parts: the file name and the extension. The file name can be up to eight characters long. The optional extension, which can be up to three characters, usually indicates the type of file. A period separates the file name and the extension. As a general rule, use only letters and numbers for file names.

4. Click on **OK**.

   This step confirms the file name. You return to the database. In the title bar, you see the file name, `CLIENTS.WDB`.

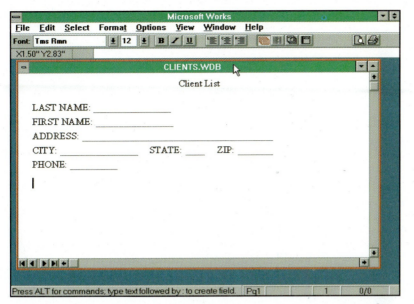

after

1. Click on **File** in the menu bar.
2. Click on the **Save** command.
3. Type the file name.
4. Click on the **OK** button.

Save often
As a general rule, you should save every 5 to 15 minutes. To save the file again, select the File Save command. (Works will not prompt you for a file name.) Until you save the database, the data is not committed to disk. You are liable to lose unsaved data—in the event of a power loss, for example.

REVIEW

To save a database

Try a shortcut
Press the Ctrl+S key combination to select the File Save command.

TASK

Open a database

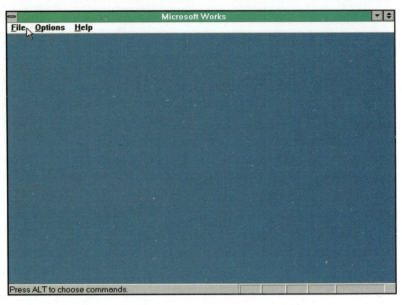

before

Oops!
If you don't want to open the file, click on the Cancel button for step 4 of the Review section.

1. **Save and close any open documents.**

   For help with this task, see *TASK: Save a document* and *TASK: Close a document window*. You can have more than one document open at a time, but you will save memory and work more quickly if you keep only the document that you are working on open.

2. **Click on File.**

   This step selects the File command. You see a list of File commands.

3. **Click on Open Existing File.**

   This step selects the Open Existing File command. You see the Open dialog box. This box displays a file list, a directory list, and other options. The insertion point is positioned in the File Name text box so that you can type a file name.

   By default, only files that have extensions starting with *w* (*.w*) are listed. If the file name has a different extension, you will not see the file. See *Using Works for Windows* for information on how to display other file types and how to change drives or directories.

4. **Type CLIENTS.**

   CLIENTS is the name of the file that you want to open. You can type the file name, if you know it, or you can point to the file name in the Files list, by using the mouse or the arrow keys. You do not have to type the extension.

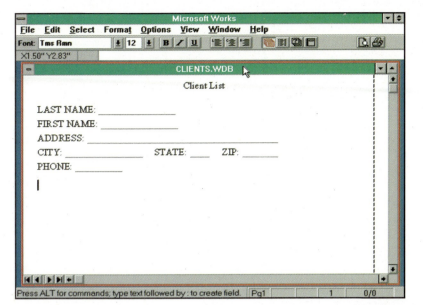

after

File not found
If you see a message box that warns `Cannot find file`, click on the OK button and double-check that you typed the file name correctly.

5. Click on **OK**.

   This step opens the database, which appears on-screen. The file name appears in the title bar.

REVIEW

To open a database

1. Click on **File** in the menu bar.
2. Click on the **Open** command.
3. Type or point to the file name.
4. Click on the **OK** button.

Try a shortcut
To open a file quickly, double-click on the file name in the Open dialog box.

Database

191

TASK

Enter a record in form view

before

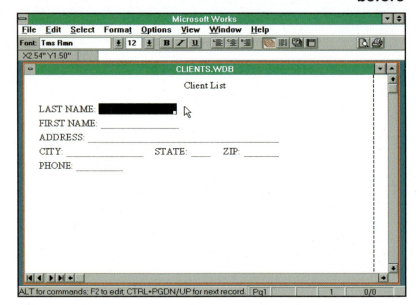

Oops!
To delete a record, see *TASK: Delete a record in form view.*

1. With the database open on-screen, click on the LAST NAME field.

   This step selects the first field in which you will begin entering the record. Be sure to click on the field; do not click on the field name.

   If the database isn't opened, open it. See *TASK: Open a database*.

2. Type **Gerdt** and press **Tab**.

   This step enters a name in the first field and highlights the next field.

3. Type **Mildred** and press **Tab**.

   This step enters a name in the FIRST NAME field and highlights the next field.

4. Type **50 South Main Street** and press **Tab**.

   This step enters the address and highlights the next field.

5. Type **Charleston** and press **Tab**.

   This step enters the city and highlights the next field.

6. Type **SC** and press **Tab**.

   This step enters the state and highlights the next field.

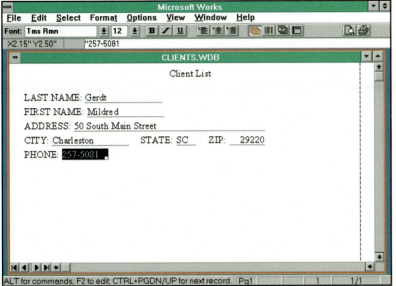

after

Make a change?
To change a record, see
TASK: Edit a record in
form view.

7. Type **29220** and press **Tab**.
   This step enters the ZIP code and highlights the next field.

8. Type **257-5081**.
   This step enters the phone number and completes the record. The record will be saved when you save the database. Be sure to save often. See TASK: Save a database.

REVIEW

1. Click on the first field.

2. Type the entry and press **Tab**.

3. Continue typing entries and pressing **Tab** until you complete all the fields.

To enter a record in form view

See a list view
To see a list view (table of all records), see TASK: Change to list view.

Database

TASK

Add a record in form view

before

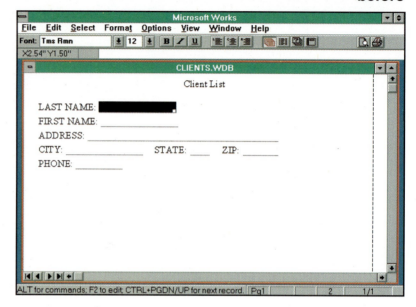

Oops!
To delete a record, see
TASK: Delete a record in form view.

1. With the last record displayed, press **Ctrl+PgDn**.
   Pressing the Ctrl+PgDn key combination displays a blank record.

2. Click on the LAST NAME field.
   This step selects the field. Be sure to click on the field; do not click on the field name.

3. Type **Ball** and press **Tab**.
   This step enters a name in the LAST NAME field and highlights the next field.

4. Type **Darlene** and press **Tab**.
   This step enters a name in the FIRST NAME field and highlights the next field.

5. Type **70 South Market Street** and press **Tab**.
   This step enters an address in the ADDRESS field and highlights the next field.

6. Type **Charleston** and press **Tab**.
   This step enters the city in the CITY field and highlights the next field.

7. Type **SC** and press **Tab**.
   This step enters the state in the STATE field and highlights the next field.

194

Easy **Works for Windows**

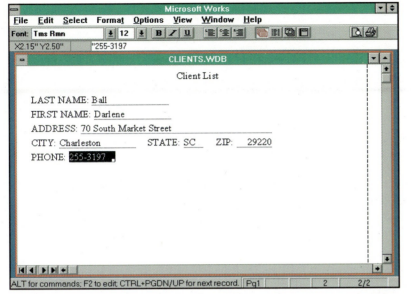

after

Insert a record
You can insert a record between two records. To do so, use the Edit Insert Record command. See *Using Works for Windows* for complete information.

8. Type **29220** and press **Tab**.

   This step enters the ZIP code in the ZIP field and highlights the next field.

9. Type **255-3197** and press **Enter**.

   This step enters the phone number in the PHONE field and completes the record.

   You also can press the Tab key to confirm the record and display a blank record. When you press Enter, the current record remains on-screen.

REVIEW

1. Press **Ctrl+PgDn** to display a blank record.
2. Click on the first field.
3. Type the entry and press **Tab**.
4. Continue typing entries and pressing **Tab** until you complete all the fields.

To add a record in form view

Make a change?
To change a record, see *TASK: Edit a record in form view.*

Database

TASK

Display a record in form view

Oops!
To display the next record, press ▶.

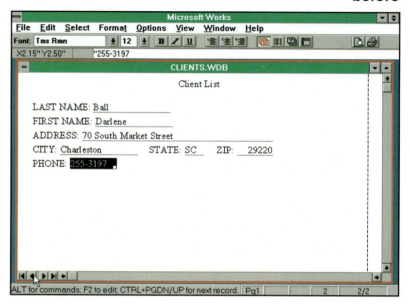

before

Click on ◀.

This step displays the previous record in the database. By default, records appear in the order you entered them.

You can click on |◀ to move to the first record. Click on ▶| to move to the last record. The last record is always a blank record.

The record number is displayed along the bottom of the status bar.

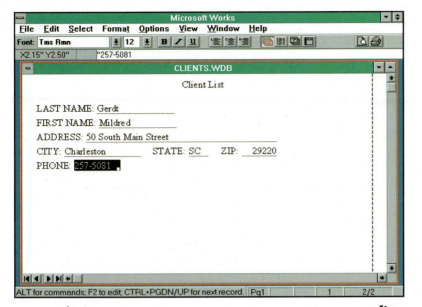

after

Use the keyboard
Press the Ctrl+PgDn key combination to move to the next record. Press the Ctrl+PgUp key combination to move to the previous record. The PgUp and PgDn keys do not work; they move around the form rather than to a different record.

REVIEW

Click on an icon to display the record that you want. You can use the following icons:

Icon	Function
|◄	Displays the first record.
◄	Displays the previous record.
►	Displays the next record.
►|	Displays the last record.

To display a record in form view

Find a record
To find a particular record, see *TASK: Find a record in form view.*

TASK

Edit a record in form view

Oops!
Follow this same procedure to restore the original text in the record.

before

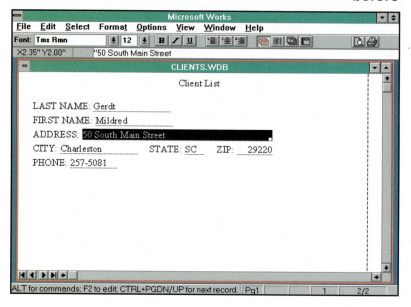

1. **Display the record for Mildred Gerdt.**
   If you don't have this record, display one that you do have. For information about displaying records, see *TASK: Display a record in form view*.

2. **Click on the ADDRESS field.**
   This step selects the field that you want to change.
   Remember to click on the field; do not click on the field name.

3. **Type 49 Rainbow Road.**
   This step changes the address.

4. **Press Enter.**
   This step confirms the change. The changes are saved when you save the database.

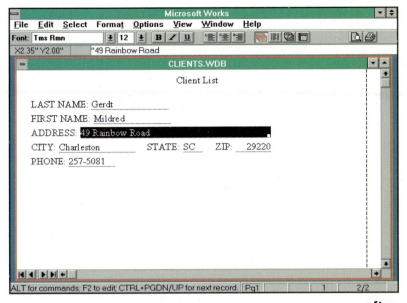
after

1. Display the record that you want to change.
2. Click on the field that you want to change.
3. Type the new entry.

REVIEW

To edit a record in form view

TASK

Find a record in form view

before

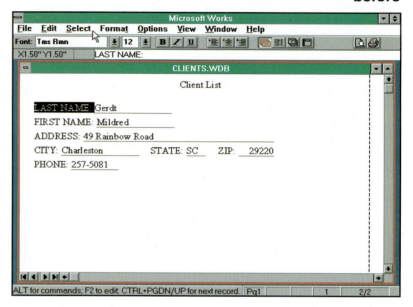

Oops!
If you see the message No match found, Works could not find the text. You may have typed the entry incorrectly. Try the search again, making sure that you type the correct characters.

1. Click on **Select**.

   This step opens the Select menu and displays Select commands.

2. Click on **Find**.

   This step selects the Find command. You see the Find dialog box, which contains the Find What text box.

3. Type **Darlene**.

   This step enters the text that you want to find. Works will search all fields in the database for the text that you enter.

4. Click on **OK**.

   This step starts the search. Works moves to the first record that matches.

Easy **Works for Windows**

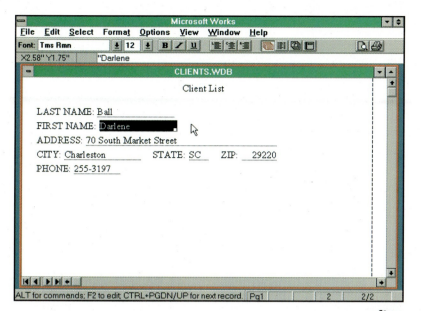

after

Repeat the search
To repeat the search, press the F7 key.

REVIEW

To find a record in form view

1. Click on **Select** in the menu bar.
2. Click on the **Find** command.
3. Type the text that you want to find.
4. Click on the **OK** button.

Use other search options
Works offers other search options. For complete information, see *Using Works for Windows*.

TASK

Delete a record in form view

before

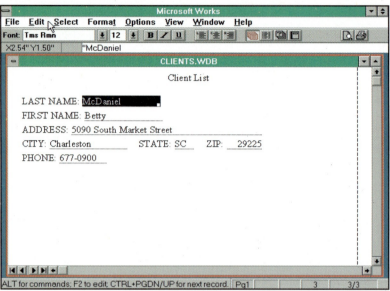

Oops!
If you change your mind, you must reenter the record. No Undelete or Undo command is available.

1. **Add the record shown in the Before screen.**
   This step adds a record so that you have one to delete. For help with this step, see *TASK: Add a record in form view*.

   If you want to delete a record you already have, display that record. See *TASK: Display a record in form view*.

2. **Click on Edit.**
   This step opens the Edit menu and displays a list of Edit commands.

3. **Click on Delete Record.**
   This step selects the Delete Record command. The record is deleted from the database.

202

Easy Works for Window

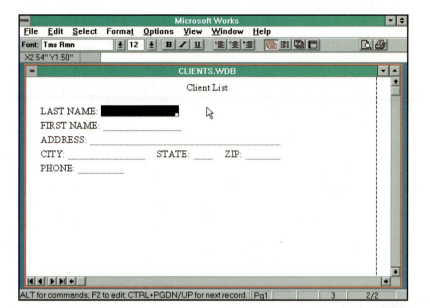
after

Be careful!
Before you select the Delete Record command, make sure that you don't need the record. The only way to recover the record is to reenter it.

1. Display the record that you want to delete.
2. Click on **Edit** in the menu bar.
3. Click on the **Delete Record** command.

REVIEW

To delete a record in form view

TASK

Change to list view

before

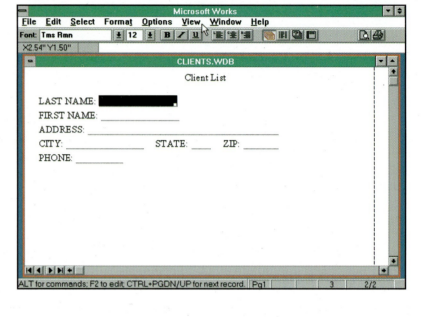

Oops!
To return to form view, select Form from the View menu.

1. **Click on View.**

   This step opens the View menu and displays a list of View commands.

2. **Click on List.**

   This step selects the List command. You see the database records in a table view—one record per row. You may not be able to see all the information in the columns because the same column width is used for all columns. (Column width is *not* the same thing as field size.)

   For information about adjusting the column width, see *TASK: Change the field width*.

   In list view, you can enter records, sort records, change field names, change field widths, edit records, and so on. The procedures are slightly different from those you learned in this section. For complete information on this view, see *Using Works for Windows*.

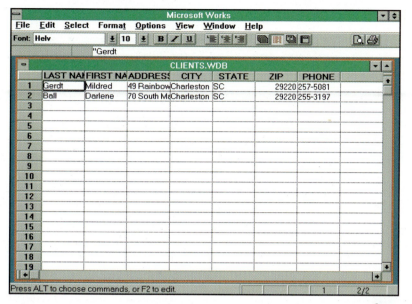
after

Try a shortcut
Press the F9 key to toggle between list view and form view.

REVIEW

1. Click on **View** in the menu bar.
2. Click on the **List** command.

To change to list view

When to use list view
Use list view when you want to work with many records at once, sort records, or delete a group of records.

TASK

Change the field width

before

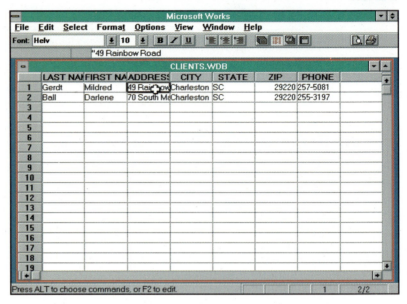

Oops!
Follow this same procedure to change the field width back to the original width (10).

1. **Display the records in list view.**
   For help with this step, see *TASK: Change to list view*. In list view, the field width for each column is set to 10. Note that the field width and the field size are *not* the same thing.

2. **Click on the ADDRESS field.**
   This step selects the field that you want to widen. You can click on any row in the column.

3. **Click on Format.**
   This step opens the Format menu. You see a list of Format commands.

4. **Click on Field Width.**
   This step selects the Field Width command. You see the Field Width dialog box. The default width is listed in the text box.

5. **Type 20.**
   This step enters a new field width.

6. **Click on OK.**
   This step confirms the field width. On-screen, the field (column) is widened.

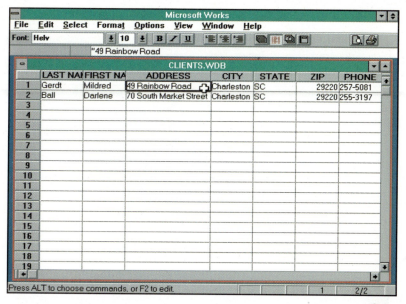
after

REVIEW

To change the field width

1. Click on the field that you want to change.
2. Click on **Format** in the menu bar.
3. Click on the **Field Width** command.
4. Type a new width.
5. Click on the **OK** button.

TASK

Add a record in list view

before

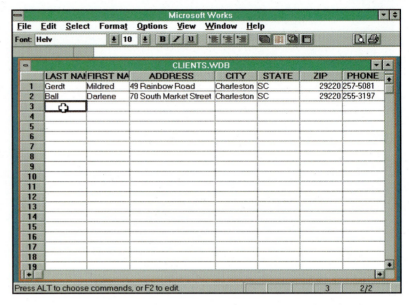

Oops!
To delete a record, see *TASK: Delete a record in list view*.

1. **Click on the first column in the first blank row.**
   This step places the insertion point in a blank row. In the Before screen, the pointer is positioned on the first blank row in the LAST NAME column.

2. **Type McDaniel and press Tab.**
   This step enters the last name and selects the next field.

3. **Type Fred and press Tab.**
   This step enters the first name and selects the next field.

4. **Type 45 South Main St and press Tab.**
   This step enters the address and selects the next field.

5. **Type Charleston and press Tab.**
   This step enters the city and selects the next field.

6. **Type SC and press Tab.**
   This step enters the state and selects the next field.

7. **Type 29220 and press Tab.**
   This step enters the ZIP code and selects the next field.

8. **Type 667-9801 and press Enter.**
   This step enters the phone number and adds the record to the database. Notice that the After screen shows the database scrolled to the right so that you can see the later fields in the database.

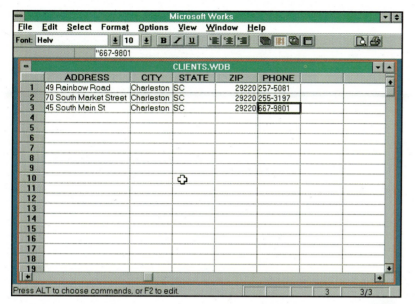
after

Make changes
To edit a record, see
TASK: Edit a record in list view.

1. Click on the first column in the first blank row.

2. Type an entry in the first field (column) and press **Tab**.

3. Continue typing entries and pressing **Tab** until you complete the record.

REVIEW

To add a record in list view

Database

TASK

Edit a record in list view

before

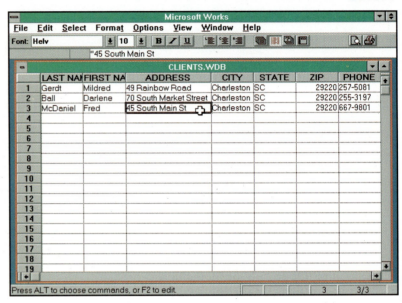

Oops!
If you change your mind and want to cancel the change, press the Esc key rather than Enter.

1. Click on the ADDRESS field for the record for Fred McDaniel.

   This step selects the field that you want to edit. The contents of this field are displayed in the list and in the formula bar.

   If you don't have this record, use another one. Click on the field that you want to change.

2. Press **F2**.

   Pressing the F2 key moves the insertion point to the formula bar so that you can edit the entry.

3. Type **reet**.

   This step changes *St* to *Street*.

4. Press **Enter**.

   This step confirms the change.

210

Easy Works for Windows

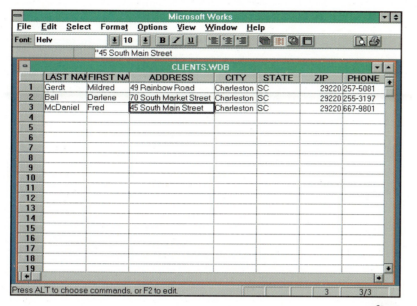

after

Overwrite the entry
To enter a completely new entry, click on the field that you want to change, type the new entry, and press Enter.

REVIEW

1. Click on the field that you want to change.
2. Press **F2**.
3. Make any changes.
4. Press **Enter**.

To edit a record in list view

TASK

Delete a record in list view

before

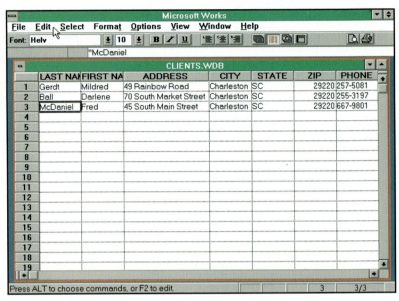

Oops!
If you change your mind, you must reenter the record. An Undelete or Undo command is not available.

1. **Click on the record for Fred McDaniel.**

   This step selects the record that you want to delete. You can click on any field in the record.

   If you don't have this record, select one that you do have. Be sure that it is a record that you want to delete.

2. **Click on Edit.**

   This step opens the Edit menu and displays a list of Edit commands.

3. **Click on Delete Record/Field.**

   This step selects the Delete Record/Field command. You see the Delete dialog box. You can choose to delete the field or the record; the record option is selected by default.

4. **Click on OK.**

   This step confirms the deletion. The record is deleted from the database.

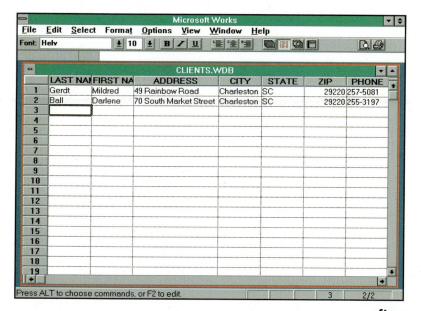

after

1. Display the record that you want to delete.
2. Click on **Edit** in the menu bar.
3. Click on the **Delete Record/Field** command.
4. Click on the **OK** button.

Be careful!
Before you select the Delete Record/Field command, make sure that you don't need the record. The only way to restore the record is to reenter it.

REVIEW

To delete a record in list view

One last caution...
Be careful not to choose to delete the field in the Delete dialog box. Doing so deletes all entries in that field.

Database

213

TASK

Sort records

Oops!
You cannot undo a sort. If you want to return to the original sort order, abandon the document.

before

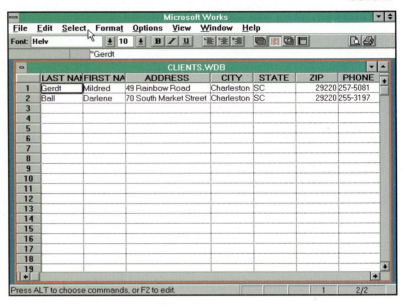

1. Display the records in list view.

   For help with this step, see *TASK: Change to list view*. You will most likely want to sort records in list view rather than form view.

2. Click on **Select**.

   This step opens the Select menu and displays Select commands.

3. Click on **Sort Records**.

   This step selects the Sort Records command. You see the Sort Records dialog box. This dialog box contains sort entries for three fields. You also can specify the sort order (ascending or descending). By default, the first field is entered as the first sort field and the sort order is ascending.

4. Click on **OK**.

   This step accepts the default settings and sorts the database.

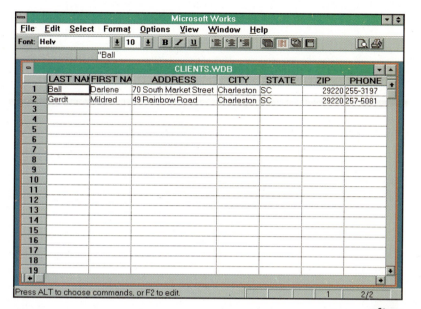

after

1. Click on **Select** in the menu bar.
2. Click on the **Sort Records** command.
3. Enter the sort fields and sort order.
4. Click on the **OK** button.

Save before you sort
It's a good idea to save the document before you sort. Then if the sort doesn't go as planned, you can return to the original document.

REVIEW

To sort records

Add an index number
If you want to return to the original sort order, you can also add a field that lists an "index" number. Use this field to number the records. Then, to return to the original order, sort on the index field.

TASK

Preview a database

before

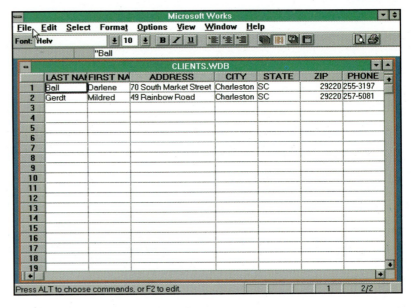

Oops!
To quit the preview, press the Esc key.

1. Click on **File**.

   This step opens the File menu. You see a list of File commands.

2. Click on **Print Preview**.

   This step selects the Print Preview command. You see a preview of your database as it will look when printed.

   To exit the preview, press the Esc key.

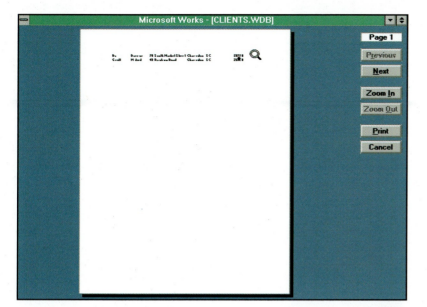

after

Use other options
You can zoom in and out of the preview and print from the preview. See *Using Works for Windows* for complete information.

REVIEW

1. Click on **File** in the menu bar.
2. Click on the **Print Preview** command.
3. Press **Esc** to exit the Preview.

To preview a database

TASK

Print a database

before

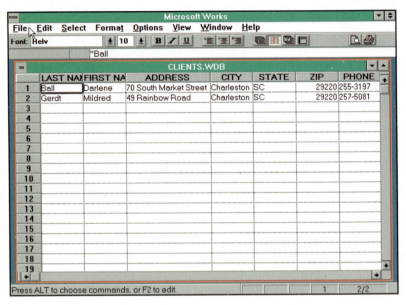

Oops!
If you don't want to print the document, click on the Cancel button for step 3.

1. Click on **File**.

   This step opens the File menu. You see a list of File commands.

2. Click on **Print**.

   This step selects the Print command. You see the Print dialog box. This dialog box enables you to specify the number of copies to print, the page range, and the text quality.

3. Click on **OK**.

   This step starts the print job.

   The After screen shows a preview of the printout, which is an on-screen representation of how the document will look when printed. (See *TASK: Preview a database*.)

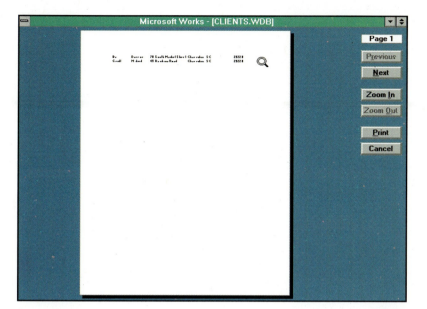

after

Try a shortcut
Press the Ctrl+P key combination to select the Print command. You also can click on the Print icon in the Toolbar. (The Print icon displays a miniature printer.)

1. Click on **File** in the menu.
2. Click on the **Print** command.
3. Click on the **OK** button.

REVIEW

To print a database

Reference

Quick Reference

Keyboard Guide

Glossary

Easy Works for Windows

Reference

Quick Reference Guide

This Quick Reference Guide covers the menu commands and keyboard shortcuts for the most commonly used Works for Windows features. The guide also includes a description of the Word Processor, Spreadsheet, and Database Toolbar.

Word Processor

The word processor tool in Works enables you to create documents such as letters, memos, resumes, and research papers.

Menu Commands and Keyboard Shortcuts

The following table lists the menu commands and keyboard shortcuts for the most commonly used word processing features:

Task Shortcut	Menu Options	Keyboard
Bold	**Format**, **Fonts & Styles**, **Bold**	**Ctrl+B**
Center	**Format**, **Indents & Spacing**, **Center**	**Ctrl+E**
Check spelling	**Options**, **Check Spelling**	
Close file	**File**, **Close**	
Copy text	**Edit**, **Copy**	**Ctrl+C**
Cut text	**Edit**, **Cut**	**Ctrl+X**
Exit	**File**, **Exit Works**	
Find	**Select**, **Find**	
Font	**Format**, **Fonts & Styles**	**Ctrl+F**
Hanging Indent	**Format**, **Indents & Spacing**	**Ctrl+H** (create) **Ctrl+G** (undo)

222

Easy Works for Windows

Task Shortcut	Menu Options	Keyboard
Help	**Help**	**F1**
Indent	**Format, Indents & Spacing**	**Ctrl+N** (create) **Ctrl+M** (undo)
Italic	**Format, Fonts & Style, Italic**	**Ctrl+I**
Left Align	**Format, Indents & Spacing**	**Ctrl+L**
Move	**Edit, Cut**; **Edit, Paste**	**Ctrl+X**; **Ctrl+V**
Open File	**File, Open Existing File**	
Page Break	**Insert, Page Break**	**Ctrl+Enter**
Paste Text	**Edit, Paste**	**Ctrl+V**
Preview	**File, Print Preview**	**Alt+F+V**
Print	**File, Print**	**Ctrl+P**
Right Align	**Format, Indents & Spacing**	**Ctrl+R**
Save	**File, Save**	**Ctrl+S**
Select...		
Word		**F8** twice
Sentence		**F8** three times
Paragraph		**F8** four times
Document		**F8** five times
Underline	**Format, Fonts & Style**	**Ctrl+U**
Undo	**Edit, Undo**	**Alt+Backspace**

Word Processor Toolbar

The following table lists the icons on the Word Processor Toolbar:

Reference

Tool	Function
Tms Rmn	Selects a font.
12	Selects a font size.
B	Makes text bold.
I	Makes text italic.
U	Underlines text.
L	Left-aligns text.
C	Centers text.
R	Right-aligns text.
J	Justifies text.
=	Single-spaces text.
=	Double-spaces text.
S	Starts the Speller.
T	Starts the Thesaurus.
🔍	Print Previews a document.
🖨	Prints a document.

Spreadsheet

The spreadsheet tool in Works enables you to create documents such as budgets, sales reports, and check registers.

Menu Commands and Keyboard Shortcuts

The following table lists the menu commands and keyboard shortcuts for the most commonly used spreadsheet features.

Task Shortcut	Menu Options	Keyboard
Bold	**Format**, **Style**	**Ctrl+B**
Center	**Format**, **Style**	**Ctrl+E**
Close File	**File**, **Close**	
Column Width	**Format**, **Column Width**	
Comma Format	**Format**, **Comma**	**Ctrl+,** (comma)
Copy Cells	**Edit**, **Copy**	**Ctrl+C**
Currency Format	**Format**, **Currency**	**Ctrl+4**
Cut Cells	**Edit**, **Cut**	**Ctrl+X**
Delete a Column	**Edit**, **Delete Row/Column**	
Delete a Row	**Edit**, **Delete Row/Column**	
Edit a Cell		**F2**
Exit	**File**, **Exit Works**	
Help	**Help**	**F1**
Insert a Column	**Edit**, **Insert Row/Column**	
Insert a Row	**Edit**, **Insert Row/Column**	

Task Shortcut	Menu Options	Keyboard
Italic	**Format**, **Style**	**Ctrl**+**I**
Left Align	**Format**, **Style**	**Ctrl**+**L**
Move	**Edit**, **Cut**; **Edit**, **Paste**	**Ctrl**+**X**; **Ctrl**+**V**
Open File	**File**, **Open Existing File**	
Paste Cells	**Edit**, **Paste**	**Ctrl**+**V**
Percent Format	**Format**, **Percent**	**Ctrl**+**5**
Preview	**File**, **Print Preview**	**Alt**+**F**+**V**
Print	**File**, **Print**	**Ctrl**+**P**
Right Align	**Format**, **Style**	**Ctrl**+**R**
Save	**File**, **Save**	**Ctrl**+**S**
Select...		
Row	**Select**, **Row**	**Ctrl**+**F8**
Column	**Select**, **Column**	**Shift**+**F8**
Entire spreadsheet	**Select**, **All**	**Ctrl**+**Shift**+**F8**
Sum formula		**Ctrl**+**M**

Spreadsheet Toolbar

The following table lists the icons on the Spreadsheet Toolbar:

Tool	Format
Tms Rmn	Selects a font.
12	Selects a font size.
B	Makes text bold.
I	Makes text italic.

Tool	Format
U	Underlines text.
	Left-aligns an entry.
	Centers an entry.
	Right-aligns an entry.
$	Formats an entry as currency.
%	Formats an entry as a percent.
,	Formats an entry with commas.
Σ	Creates a sum formula.
	Creates a new chart.
	Print previews a spreadsheet.
	Prints a spreadsheet.

Database

The database tool in Works enables you to create documents such as inventory reports, personnel reports, and client listings.

Menu Commands and Keyboard Shortcuts

The following table lists the menu commands and keyboard shortcuts for the most commonly used database features.

Task Shortcut	*Menu Options*	*Keyboard*
Bold	**Format, Character**	**Ctrl+B**
Center	**Format, Paragraph**	**Ctrl+E**
Close file	**File, Close**	
Cut a Record	**Edit, Cut**	**Ctrl+X**
Copy a Record	**Edit, Copy**	**Ctrl+C**
Exit	**File, Exit Works**	
Find a record	**Edit, Find**	
Font	**Format, Character**	**Ctrl+F**
Form view	**View, Form**	**F9**
Help	**Help**	**F1**
Italic	**Format, Character**	**Ctrl+I**
Left Align	**Format, Paragraph**	**Ctrl+L**
List view	**View, List**	**F9**
Move	**Edit, Cut; Edit, Paste**	**Ctrl+X; Ctrl+V**
Open file	**File, Open Existing File**	
Paste text	**Edit, Paste**	**Ctrl+V**
Preview	**File, Print Preview**	**Alt+F+V**
Print	**File, Print**	**Ctrl+P**
Right Align	**Format, Paragraph**	**Ctrl+R**
Save	**File, Save**	**Ctrl+S**
Sort Record	**Select, Sort Records**	
Underline	**Format, Character**	**Ctrl+U**

Database Toolbar

The following table lists the icons on the Database Toolbar:

Tool	Function
Helv	Selects a font.
10	Selects a font size.
B	Makes a field bold.
I	Makes a field italic.
U	Underlines a field.
	Left-aligns a field.
	Centers a field.
	Right-aligns a field.
	Displays records in form view.
	Displays records in list view.
	Switches to query view.
	Switches to report view.
	Print previews a database.
	Prints a database.

Reference

229

Keyboard Guide

Instead of using the mouse with Works for Windows, you can use the keyboard. This section covers some basic keyboard operations. The Quick Reference guide also lists keyboard shortcuts. For complete instructions on using the keyboard, see *Using Works for Windows*.

To open a menu

Press the **Alt** key, and then type the underlined letter in the menu name.

To select a menu command

1. Use ↑ or ↓ to move to the command that you want to open.
2. Press **Enter**.

Or

Type the underlined letter in the menu command name.

To select a text box in a dialog box

Press and hold down the **Alt** key; then type the underlined letter in the text box.

To make an entry in the box, type the entry and then press **Enter**.

To select a check box or option button in a dialog box

Press and hold down the **Alt** key; then type the underlined letter in the check box or option button.

To select an item in a list box

Press and hold down the **Alt** key; then type the underlined letter in the list box. Use the arrow keys to select the item.

To select text

Press and hold down the **Shift** key; then use the arrow keys to highlight the text. (Press the arrow key that points in the direction that you want to highlight the text.)

To select cells in a spreadsheet

Press and hold down the **Shift** key; then use the arrow keys to highlight cells.

Glossary

cell The intersection of any column and row. Each cell in a spreadsheet has a unique address. A cell address is formed by combining the column and row locations into one description. For example, A8 describes the intersection of column A and row 8.

chart A visual representation of your data. You can display selected data using one of many chart types—bar chart, pie chart, line chart, and so on.

Clipboard A temporary storage place for text or graphics. When you cut or copy text or graphics, the item is stored in the Clipboard. The Clipboard is a Windows feature.

Control menu box The hyphen or little box that appears at the left end of the title bar of a window. Double-clicking on this box closes the window.

default Standard Works settings that are in effect each time you start the program.

dialog box An on-screen window that displays further command options. Many times a dialog box reminds you of the consequences or results of a command and asks you to confirm that you want to go ahead with the action.

directory An index to the files stored on disk or a list of files. A directory is similar to a file cabinet; you can group files together in directories.

document window The area in which you type text. You can have more than one document window open at once.

DOS An acronym for *disk operating system*. DOS manages the details of your system—storing and retrieving programs and files.

field One item in a database record. For instance, in a phone book database, the entry for the last name would be one field. The entry for the first name would be in another field.

file The various individual reports, memos, databases, letters, and so on that you store on your hard drive (or floppy disk) for future use. In addition, the actual Works program is stored in a file.

file name The name that you assign a file when you store it to disk. A file name consists of two parts: the root and the extension. The root can be up to eight characters long. The optional extension can be up to three characters long and usually indicates the file type. The root and extension are separated by a period. MEMO.WPS is a valid file name. MEMO is the root, and WPS is the extension.

floppy disk drive A door into your computer. The floppy disk drive allows you to put information onto the computer—onto the hard drive—and to take information off the computer—onto a floppy disk.

font The style, size, and typeface of a set of characters.

formula An entry that performs a calculation on two or more values or series of values in cells.

form view A view that displays your database one record at a time.

function A built-in formula supplied with Works. Functions perform specialized calculations, such as loan payments.

hard disk drive The device within your system unit that stores the programs and files with which you work. A hard disk drive is similar to a floppy disk drive, except that a hard disk stores more information, is usually not removable, and works much more quickly.

hard return A code inserted into the document when you press Enter. A hard return is used to end a line and insert a blank line.

icon A picture that represents a group window, an application, a document, or other elements within windows.

insertion point A vertical line that indicates the place where you begin typing text, deleting text, selecting text, and so on.

label Text, such as a title, that is added to a database form.

list view A view that displays several records on-screen at once. The records are displayed in rows.

menu An on-screen list of Works options.

Microsoft Windows An operating environment that provides a graphical interface (rather than DOS). A graphical interface lets you learn a computer program more intuitively and use a computer program more easily. With Microsoft Windows you can manage your computer system—run programs, copy files, and so on.

mouse An input device, like a keyboard, that enables you to move the cursor on-screen, select menu commands, and perform other operations.

mouse pointer The graphic that appears on-screen and indicates the location of the insertion point. You can move the mouse pointer around on-screen by sliding the mouse on the top of your desk.

numeric format The way in which values are displayed. You can display dollar signs, decimal points, commas, percentages, and so on.

path name The route, through directories, to a program or document file. For instance, the path C:\MSWORKS\DATA\REPORT.WPS includes these elements: the disk drive (C:); the root directory (indicated by a backslash); the next directory (MSWORKS); the next directory, which is a directory within the first directory (DATA); and the file name (REPORT.WPS).

query A process that requests information from a database, like a search. For instance, you might query for all clients who live in Georgia and have expressed interest in a certain product.

range A group of selected cells. A range can be a cell, a row, a column, or any rectangular area of columns and rows. After you select a range, you can perform many operations on that range.

range coordinates The elements that define a range. Works identifies a range as follows: The first element is the location of the uppermost left cell in the range; the second element is the location of the lowermost right cell in the range. For instance, the range A1:C3 includes the cells A1, A2, A3, B1, B2, B3, C1, C2, and C3.

record All the information in a database about one person, event, or product. For instance, in a phone book database, the entries for first name, last name, address, and phone number would comprise one record.

root directory The main directory. All other directories are contained in the root directory.

Ruler An on-screen graphic that allows you to make formatting changes (change tabs, indents, and margins) in the word processor. You can turn on or off the display of the Ruler.

scroll bars The bars at the bottom and right of a window. At the ends of the bars are scroll arrows; click on the arrow to scroll the window in that direction.

spreadsheet All the data and formatting information you enter on-screen. Works and your operating system keep track of spreadsheets by storing them on disk in files.

status bar The bottom line of the Works screen. This bar displays status indicators such as the current location of the insertion point.

title bar The area of the document or application window that displays the name of the document (or application).

tool One part of the Works for Windows package. Works includes a word processor tool, a spreadsheet tool, a chart tool, a draw tool, and a database tool.

Toolbar An on-screen area that displays buttons you can use to access commonly used features.

window A rectangular area on-screen in which you view an application or a document. A window can contain icons that represent applications, actual applications, or a document you have created in an application.

word wrap A Works feature that eliminates the need to press Enter each time you reach the right margin of a document. Instead, Works moves ("wraps") the words to the next line automatically.

Index

Easy Works for Windows

Index

Symbols

\# (number signs), 123
↓ key, 34
← key, 34
→ key, 34
... (ellipsis), 31
: (colons), 175
<< (soft page break), 71
¶ (paragraph mark), 66

A

active windows, 50-51
aligning text, spreadsheets, 148-149
Alignment area, 92-93
Alt+Backspace (undo) key combination, 81
Alt+F4 (exit) key combination, 57
arranging windows, 51-53
arrow keys, 19, 22, 35
AT keyboard, 20
auto-sum tool, 127

B

Backspace key, 23
blank lines, inserting, 66-67
bold text
   spreadsheet tool, 152-153
   word processor tool, 6, 82-83

C

calculations, spreadsheet tool, 6
canceling printing, 113
Cannot find file message, 109, 165, 191
cells, 116-117, 231
   entries, 128-135
   overwriting, 129
   selecting, 18, 231
centering text
   spreadsheet tool, 149
   word processor tool, 92-93
chart tool, 2, 24
charts, 231
check boxes, 32, 230
Check Spelling (Options menu) command, 96-99
check spelling, *see* spelling check
Clear (Edit menu) command, 140-141
clearing ranges, spreadsheet tool, 140-141

clicking mouse, 19, 42-43
Clipboard, 76-77, 138-139, 231
Close (File menu) command, 54-55
closing windows, 29, 45, 53-55
Column Width (Format menu) command, 146-147
Column Width dialog box, 146-147
columns (spreadsheets), 116-117
   deleting, 156-157
   inserting, 154-155
   width, 146-147
commands
   Close (File menu), 54-55
   Create New File (File menu), 48-49
   database tool, 227-228
      Delete Field (Edit menu), 186-187
      Delete Record (Edit menu), 202-203
      Delete Record/Field (Edit menu), 212-213
      Field Size (Format menu), 185
      Field Width (Format menu), 206-207
      Find (Select menu), 200-201
      Insert Record (Edit menu), 195
      List (View menu), 204-205
      Open Existing File (File menu), 190-191
      Position Field (Edit menu), 183
      Print (File menu), 218-219
      Print Preview (File menu), 216-217
      Save (File menu), 188-189
      Sort Records (Select menu), 214-215
   dialog boxes, 31
   ellipsis (...), 31
   Exit Works (File menu), 56-57
   Index (Help menu), 46-47
   selecting
      keyboard, 230
      menu bar, 28
      menus, 31
      mouse, 18
      Toolbar, 28
   Show All Characters (Options menu), 66
   spreadsheet tool, 225-226
      Clear (Edit menu), 140-141
      Column Width (Format menu), 146-147
      Copy (Edit menu), 132-133, 138-139, 144-145
      Currency (Format menu), 150-151

Cut (Edit menu), 134-135, 142-143
Delete Row/Column (Edit menu), 156-157, 160-161
Insert Row/Column (Edit menu), 158-159
Insert/Row Column (Edit menu), 154-155
Open Existing File (File menu), 164-165
Paste (Edit menu), 132-135, 144-145
Print (File menu), 168-169
Print Preview (File menu), 166-167
Save (File menu), 162-163
Style (Format menu), 148-149, 152-153
Tile (Window menu), 52-53
win (start Windows), 42-43
word processor tool, 222-223
Check Spelling (Options menu), 96-99
Copy (Edit menu), 76-77
Cut (Edit menu), 78-79
Find (Select menu), 100-101
Font & Style (Format menu), 82-91
Indents & Spacing (Format menu), 92-95
Open Exising File (File menu), 108–109
Page Break (Insert menu), 70-71
Paste (Edit menu), 79
Print (File menu), 112-113
Print Preview (File menu), 110-111
Replace (Select menu), 102-103
Save (File menu), 106-107
Undo (Edit menu), 80-81
computer system, 16-18
see also hardware; individual listings
Control menu box, 29, 231
Copy (Edit menu) command, 76-77, 132-133, 138-139, 144-145
copying
cell entries, 132-133
formulas, 144-145
ranges, 138-139
text, word processor tool, 76-77
correcting errors, word processor tool, 4-5
Create New File (File menu) command, 48-49

creating
databases, 172-173
documents, 46-47, 60-61
spreadsheets, 116-117
Ctrl+B (bold) key combination, 83, 153
Ctrl+C (copy) key combination, 77, 133, 145
Ctrl+E (center text) key combination, 93
Ctrl+End key combination, 34
Ctrl+Enter (page break) key combination, 71
Ctrl+Home (move insertion point), 34, 96-97
Ctrl+I (italic) key combination, 85
Ctrl+N (indent) key combination, 95
Ctrl+P (print) key combination, 113, 218-219
Ctrl+P (print) key combinations, 169
Ctrl+PgDn, 197
Ctrl+PgUp, 197
Ctrl+S (save) key combination, 107, 163, 189
Ctrl+U (underline) key combination, 87
Ctrl+V (paste) key combination, 77, 79, 133, 145
Ctrl+X (cut) key combination, 79, 135
Currency (Format menu) command, 150-151
Currency dialog box, 150-151
Cut (Edit menu) command, 78-79, 134-135, 142-143

D

database tool, 2, 24
commands, 227-228
Delete Field (Edit menu), 186-187
Delete Record (Edit menu), 202-203
Field Width (Format menu), 206-207
Find (Select menu), 200-201
Insert Record (Edit menu), 195
List (View menu), 204-205
Open Existing File (File menu), 190-191
Position Field (Edit menu), 183
Print (File menu), 218-219

    Print Preview (File menu),
      216-217
    Save (File menu), 188-189
    Sort Records (Select menu),
      214-215
  creating databases, 172-173
  document window, 27
  documents, 3
    opening, 190-191
    saving, 188-189
  key combinations, 227-228
  list view, 193, 204-205
  printing, 218-219
  see also databases
Database Toolbar icons, 229
databases
  creating, 172-173
  entries, overwriting, 211
  fields, 232
    adding, 178-179
    deleting, 186-187
    moving, 182-183
    names, 176-177
    names, editing, 180-181
    sizing, 184-185
    width, 206-207
  form view (records), 233
    adding, 194-195
    deleting, 202-203
    displaying, 196-197
    editing, 198-199
    entering, 192-193
    finding, 200-201
  labels, 174, 233
  list view (records), 193, 204-205,
    233
    adding, 208-209
    deleting, 212-213
    editing, 210-211
  opening, 190-191
  printing, 216-219
  queries, 234
  rearranging, 183
  saving, 188-189
  sorting records, 214-215
  see also database tool
date prompt, 42-43
dates, spreadsheets, 122-123
decimal places, 150-151
defaults, 231
Del key, 19
Delete dialog box, 157, 161,
  212-213
Delete Field (Edit menu) command,
  186-187
Delete key, 24
Delete Record (Edit menu)
  command, 202-203

Delete Record/Field (Edit menu)
  command, 212-213
Delete Row/Column (Edit menu)
  command, 156-157, 160-161
deleting
  blank lines, 66-67
  characters, 62-63
  columns, spreadsheets, 156-157
  fields, databases, 186-187
  formulas, spreadsheets, 144-145
  labels, databases, 174
  records, databases, 202-203,
    212-213
  rows, spreadsheets, 160-161
  text, word processor tool, 74-75
dialog boxes, 32-34, 231
dictionary (checking spelling), 96-99
directories, 232, 234, 235
disk drives, 16-17, 232-233
disk operating system (DOS), 232
displaying
  document windows, 52-53
  records, databases, 196-197
  windows, 49, 51
document window, 26, 232
  application title bar, 28
  arranging, 52-53
  closing, 45, 53-55
  database tool, 26-27
  document title bar, 28
  menu bar, 28
  scroll bar, 28, 235
  spreadsheet tool, 26-27
  status bar, 28, 235
  switching, 50-51
  title bar, 235
  Toolbar, 28
  word processor tool, 27-28, 60-61
  workspace, 28-29
documents
  combining paragraphs, 68-69
  creating, 46-47
    database tool, 3
    spreadsheet tool, 2-3
    word processor tool, 60-61
  editing, 5
  formatting, 6
  opening
    database tool, 190-191
    multiple, 49
    spreadsheet tool, 164-165
    word processor tool, 108-109
  previewing, 110-111, 166-167
  printing
    spreadsheet tool, 168-169
    word processing tool, 112-113
  retrieving, 34

saving, 34, 57
    database tool, 188-189
    word processing tool, 106-107
spelling check, word processor tool, 5
spreadsheet tool, *see* spreadsheets
switching, 49
text, 5
DOS (disk operating system), 232
dragging mouse, 19
draw tool, 2, 25
drop-down list box, 34

E

editing
    cell entries, 128-129
    documents, 5
    fields, names, 180-181
    records, 198-199, 210-211
ellipsis (...), 31
End key, 22
Enhanced keyboard, 20
entering
    dates, spreadsheets, 122-123
    formulas, spreadsheets, 124-125
    numbers, spreadsheets, 120-121
    records, databases, 192-193
    text
        spreadsheet tool, 118-119
        word processor tool, 62-63
erasing
    cell entries, spreadsheets, 130-131
    ranges, spreadsheets, 140-141
errors, correcting, word processor tool, 4-5
Esc key, 23
Exit Windows dialog box, 56-57
Exit Works (File menu) command, 56-57
exiting, Works for Windows, 43, 56-57
extensions, file names, 106-107, 162-165

F

F7 (search) key, 101
F9 (switch between list and form view), 205
Field Size (Format menu) command, 185
Field Width (Format menu) command, 206-207

Field Width dialog box, 206-207
fields (databases), 232
    adding, 178-179
    cells, mouse, 18
    deleting, 186-187
    moving, 182-183
    names, 176-177, 180-181
    selecting, mouse, 18
    sizing, 184-185
    width, 206-207
File Name text box, 108-109
file names, 106-109, 162-165, 232
files, 232, 234
Find (Select menu) command, 100-101, 200-201
Find dialog box, 100-103, 200-201
finding records (databases), 7, 197, 200-201
floppy disk drives, 232
Font & Style (Format menu) command, 82-91
Font & Style dialog box, 82-91
fonts, 88-91, 232
form view records (databases), 233
    adding, 194-195
    deleting, 202-203
    displaying, 196-197
    editing, 198-199
    entering, 192-193
    finding, 200-201
formats (spreadsheets), 150-151, 234
formatting
    data, spreadsheet tool, 7
    documents, 6
    ranges, spreadsheets, 150-151
    text, 82-87
    undoing, 88-89
formula bar, 116-117
formulas (spreadsheets), 232
    copying, 144-145
    deleting, 144-145
    entering, 124-125
function keys, 19-21, 101, 205
functions, 233
    spreadsheets, 126-127
    SUM, 125

G-H

group icons, 42-43

hard disk drive, 16-17, 233
hard return, 67, 233
hardware
    floppy disk drive, 16-17
    hard disk drive, 16-17
    keyboard, 16-17
    monitor, 16-17

mouse, 17-18
printer, 17
system unit, 16-17
help, 46-47
Home key, 22

I-J

icons, 233
    group, 42-43
    spreadsheet tool, 48-49
    toolbar
        database, 229
        Print, 169
        Print Preview, 167
        right-align, 149
        spreadsheet, 226-227
        word processor, 223-224
indenting text, 94-95
Indents & Spacing (Format menu) command, 92-95
Indents & Spacing dialog box, 92-95
Index (Help menu) command, 46-47
index number (sorting), 215
Ins key, 19
Insert dialog box, 155, 159
Insert Record (Edit menu) command, 195
Insert Row/Column (Edit menu) command, 154-155, 158-159
inserting
    columns, spreadsheets, 154-155
    lines, blank, 66-67
    records between records, 195
    rows, spreadsheets, 158-159
    text, word processor tool, 64-65
insertion point, 35, 63, 96-97, 233
installing Works for Windows, 43
italic text, 6, 84-85

K

key combinations
    Alt+Backspace (undo), 81
    Alt+F4 (exit), 57
    Ctrl+B (bold), 83, 153
    Ctrl+C (copy), 77, 133, 145
    Ctrl+E (center text), 93
    Ctrl+End, 35
    Ctrl+Enter (page break), 71
    Ctrl+Home, 35
    Ctrl+I (italic), 85
    Ctrl+N (indent), 95
    Ctrl+P (print), 113, 169, 218-219
    Ctrl+PgDn, 197
    Ctrl+PgUp, 197
    Ctrl+S (save), 107, 163, 189
    Ctrl+U (underline), 87
    Ctrl+V (paste), 77-79, 133, 145
    Ctrl+X (cut), 79, 135
    database tool, 227-228
    spreadsheet tool, 225-226
    word processor tool, 222-223
keyboard, 16-17, 34
    arrow keys, 22, 19
    AT, 20
    Backspace, 23
    Del key, 19, 23
    editing keys, 19
    End key, 22
    Enhanced, 20
    Esc, 23
    function keys, 19, 21
    Home, 22
    Ins key, 19
    modifier keys, 19
    opening menus, 230
    PC (original), 20
    PgDn, 22
    PgUp, 22
    selecting
        check boxes, 230
        commands, 230
        option buttons, 230
        text, 73, 231
        text boxes, 230
    shortcut keys, 20-21

L

labels (databases), 174-175, 233
lines (blank), inserting, 66-67
List (View menu) command, 204-205
list boxes, 33, 230
list view (databases), 193, 204-205, 233
    adding records, 208-209
    deleting records, 212-213
listing of tasks, 38-40

M

maximizing windows, 30, 52-53
menu bars, 28
menus, 233
    commands, selecting, 31
    Control, 29, 231
    opening, keyboard, 230

messages
    Cannot find file, 109, 165, 191
    No match found, 100-105, 200-201
    Replace exising file?, 162-163, 188-189
Microsoft Windows, 233
monitor, 16-17, 42-43
mouse, 17-18, 233
    clicking, 19, 42-43
    column width adjustment, 147
    dragging, 19
    insertion point, moving, 35
    pointer, 18-19, 234
    selecting, 18
moving
    cell entries, spreadsheet tool, 134-135
    fields, databases, 182-183
    insertion point, 34, 96-97
    ranges, spreadsheets, 135, 142-143
    text, word processor tool, 78-79
    windows, 30
multiplication (*) math operator, 124-125

N

names
    fields, databases, 176-177
    files, 106-107
navigating documents, 5
negative numbers, 121
No match found message, 100-105, 200-201
number signs (#), 123
numbers, 120-121
numeric format, 23

O

Open dialog box, 108-109, 164-165
Open Existing File (File menu) command, 108-109, 164-165, 190-191
opening
    databases, 190-191
    documents
        multiple, 49
        word processor tool, 108-109
    menus, keyboard, 230
    spreadsheets, 164-165
option buttons, 34, 230

overwriting
    cells, spreadsheets, 129
    entries, databases, 211
    text, word processor tool, 65

P

Page Break (Insert menu) command, 70-71
page breaks, 70-71
paragraph mark (¶), 66
paragraphs, combining, 68-69
Paste (Edit menu) command, 79, 132-135, 144-145
path names, 234
PC keyboard, 20
pointers, 18-19, 234
Position Field (Edit menu) command, 183
previewing
    databases, 216-217
    documents, 110-111
    spreadsheets, 166-167
    zooming, 167, 217
Print (File menu) command, 112-113, 168-169, 218-219
Print dialog box, 112-113, 168-169, 218-219
Print icon, 169
Print Preview (File menu) command, 110-111, 166-167, 216-217
Print Preview icon, 167
printers, 17
printing
    canceling, 113
    databases, 216-219
    documents, word processing tool, 112-113
    previewing
        databases, 216-217
        spreadsheets, 166-167
        word processor tool, 110-111
    spreadsheets, 168-169
prompts, date and time, 42-43

Q-R

queries, 234

ranges (spreadsheets), 234
    clearing, 140-141
    coordinates, 234
    copying, 138-139
    erasing, 140-141
    formatting, 150-151
    moving, 135, 142-143
    selecting, 136-137

rearranging
    databases, 183
    spreadsheets, 143
    text, word processor tool, 5
records (databases), 234
    changing, 7
    form view
        adding, 194-195
        deleting, 202-208
        displaying, 196-197
        editing, 198-199
        entering, 192-193
    finding, 197
        database tool, 7, 200-201
        repeating search, 201
    list view
        adding, 208-209
        deleting, 212-213
        editing, 210-211
    inserting between records, 195
    sorting, 7, 214-215
references, 13
Replace (Select menu) command, 102-103
Replace dialog box, 102-103
Replace existing file? message, 162-163, 188-189
Replace With What text box, 102-103
replacing text, 6, 102-105
resize box, 184-185
resizing windows, 31
restoring text, 5, 74-75, 78-79
retrieving documents, 35
returns, 67, 233
root directory, 235
rows (spreadsheets), 116-117
    deleting, 160-161
    inserting, 158-159
ruler, 60-61, 235

S

Save (File menu) command, 106-107, 162-163, 188-189
Save As dialog box, 106–107, 162-163, 188-189
saving
    databases, 188-189
    documents, 35, 57, 106-107
    spreadsheets, 162-163
scroll bar, 28, 235
scrolling windows, 30
search string, 100-101
searching, 100-101, 201
selecting
    cells, mouse, 18
    check boxes, keyboard, 230
    commands
        keyboard, 230
        menu bar, 28
        menus, 32
    items, list boxes, 230
    option buttons, 230
    ranges, 136-137
    text
        keyboard, 231
        mouse, 18
        word processor tool, 72-73
    text boxes, 230
    tools, 44-45, 60-61
shortcut keys, *see* key combinations
Show All Characters (Options menu) command, 66
soft page break, 71
soft returns, 67
SolutionSeries, 42-43
Sort Records (Select menu) command, 214-215
Sort Records dialog box, 214-215
sorting records (databases), 7, 214-215
spelling check, 5, 96-99
Spelling dialog box, 97-99
splitting paragraphs, 68-69
spreadsheet tool, 2, 24, 116-117
    calculating, 6
    chart tool, 24
    Clipboard, 138-139
    commands, 225-226
        Clear (Edit menu), 140-141
        Column Width (Format menu), 146-147
        Copy (Edit menu), 132-133, 138-139, 144-145
        Currency (Format menu), 150-151
        Cut (Edit menu), 134-135, 142-143
        Delete Row/Column (Edit menu), 156-157, 160-161
        Insert Row/Column (Edit menu), 154-155, 158-159
        Open Existing File (File menu), 164-165
        Paste (Edit menu), 132-135, 144-145
        Print (File menu), 168-169
        Print Preview (File menu), 166-167
        Save (File menu), 162-163
        Style (Format menu), 148-149, 152-153
    document window, 27
    documents, *see* spreadsheets
    formatting data, 7, 122-124
    icon, 48-49

key combinations, 225-226
rearranging data, 7, 143
recalculating, 6
repeating data, 7
see also spreadsheets
Spreadsheet Toolbar icons, 226-227
spreadsheets, 235
(number signs), 123
cell entries
bold, 152-153
copying, 132-133
editing, 128-129
erasing, 130-131
moving, 134-135
cells, 116-117, 231
columns, 116-117
deleting, 156-157
inserting, 154-155
width, 146-147
creating, 116-117
dates, entering, 122-123
formula bar, 116-117
formulas, 124-125, 144-145, 232
functions, 126-127, 233
numbers, 120-121
opening, 164-165
previewing, 166-167
printing, 166-169
ranges, 234
clearing, 140-141
coordinates, 234
copying, 138-139
erasing, 140-141
formatting, 150-151
moving, 135, 142-143
selecting, 136-137
rows, 116-117
deleting, 160-161
inserting, 158-159
saving, 162-163
SUM function, 125
text
aligning, 148-149
bold, 152-153
centering, 149
entering, 118-119
see also spreadsheet tool
starting Works for Windows, 42-43, 60-61
Startup dialog box, 44-45
status bar, 28, 235
Style (Format menu) command, 148-149, 152-153
Style dialog box, 148-149, 152-153
Styles area, 82-87, 152-153
SUM function, 125
system unit, 16-17

T–U

tasks, listing, 38-40
text
spreadsheets
alignment, 148-149
bold, 152-153
centering, 149
entering, 118-119
word processor tool
bold, 6, 82-83
centering, 92-93
copying, 76-77
deleting, 74-75
entering, 62-63
indenting, 94-95
inserting, 64-65
italic, 6, 84-85
moving, 78-79
overwriting, 65
rearranging, 6, 102-105
replacing, 6, 102-105
restoring, 74-75, 78-79
searching for, 6, 100-101
selecting, 72-73
underlining, 86-87
fonts, 88-91, 232
insertion point, 63
labels, 233
selecting
keyboard, 231
mouse, 18
word wrap, 67
text boxes, 32, 230
Tile (Window menu) command, 52-53
time prompt, 42-43
title bar, 28, 235
Toolbar, 28, 116-117, 235
auto-sum tool, 127
database, icons, 229
font, 89, 91
formatting ranges, 151
Print Preview icon, 167
selecting commands, 28
spreadsheet, icons, 226-227
word processor, icons, 223-224
tools, 235
chart, 2, 25
database, 2, 25
draw, 2, 25
help, 47
selecting, 44-45, 60-61
spreadsheet, 2, 24
word processor, 2, 24
turning on
computer, 42-43
monitor, 42-43

underlining text, word processor tool, 86-87
Undo (Edit menu) command, 64-65, 80-81

W-Z

win (start Windows) command, 42-43
Window menu, 50-51
Windows, 42-43, 46-47, 233
windows, 29, 235
    active, 50-51
    arranging, 51
    closing, 29, 53
    Control menu box, 30
    displaying, 49, 51
    document, 26, 232
        arranging, 52-53
        closing, 54-55
        database tool, 27
        spreadsheet tool, 27
        switching, 50-51
    Help, 46-47
    maximizing, 30, 52-53
    moving, 30
    resizing, 30
    scroll bars, 235
    scrolling, 32
    status bar, 235
    title bar, 235
word processor tool, 2, 24
    blank lines, inserting, 66-67
    Clipboard, 76-77
    commands, 222-223
        Check Spelling (Options menu), 96-99
        Copy (Edit menu), 76-77
        Cut (Edit menu), 78-79
        Find (Select menu), 100-101
        Font & Style (Format menu), 82-91
        Indents & Spacing (Format menu), 92-95
        Open Exising File (File menu), 108-109
        Page Break (Insert menu), 70-71
        Paste (Edit menu), 79
        Print (File menu), 112-113
        Print Preview (File menu), 110-111
        Replace (Select menu), 102-103
        Save (File menu), 106-107
        Undo (Edit menu), 80-81

correcting errors, 4-5
document window, 26
documents, 2
    creating, 60-61
    editing, 5
    formatting, 6
    navigating, 5
    opening, 108-109
    page breaks, 70-71
    previewing, 110-111
    saving, 106-107
    spelling check, 5
font size, 90-91
hard return, 67
key combinations, 222-223
printing, 6, 112-113
Ruler, 235
soft return, 67
spelling check, 96-99
splitting paragraphs, 68-69
text
    bold, 6, 82-83
    centering, 92-93
    copying, 76-77
    deleting, 74-75
    entering, 62-63
    fonts, 88-89
    indenting, 94-95
    inserting, 64-65
    italic, 6
    moving, 78-79
    overwriting, 65
    rearranging, 5
    replacing, 6, 102-105
    restoring, 5, 74-75, 78-79
    searching for, 6, 100-101
    selecting, 72-73
    word wrap, 67, 235
Word Processor Toolbar icons, 223-224
word wrap, 67, 235
Works for Windows
    exiting, 43, 56-57
    installing, 43
    starting, 42-43, 60-61
workspace, 28-29

zooming, 167, 217